Mississippi Black Paper

CIVIL RIGHTS IN MISSISSIPPI
Trent Brown, General Editor

Mississippi Black Paper

FOREWORD BY **Reinhold Niebuhr**
INTRODUCTION BY **Hodding Carter III**
INTRODUCTION TO THE NEW EDITION BY **Jason Morgan Ward**

UNIVERSITY PRESS OF MISSISSIPPI • JACKSON

www.upress.state.ms.us

Designed by Peter D. Halverson

The University Press of Mississippi is a member of the
Association of American University Presses.

Original text © 1965, by Misseduc Foundation, Inc. Reprinted by the University Press
of Mississippi 2017 by permission of Elisabeth Sifton and Hodding Carter III.

Compiled by the Council of Federated Organizations.

Introduction copyright © 2017 University Press of Mississippi
All rights reserved
Manufactured in the United States of America

First UPM printing 2017
∞

Library of Congress Cataloging-in-Publication Data

Names: Niebuhr, Reinhold, 1892–1971, writer of foreword. | Carter, Hodding,
  writer of introduction. | Ward, Jason Morgan, writer of introduction.
Title: Mississippi black paper / foreword by Reinhold Niebuhr; introduction
  by Hodding Carter III; introduction to the new edition by Jason Morgan
  Ward.
Description: Jackson: University Press of Mississippi, [2017] | Series:
  Civil rights in Mississippi | "Original text © 1965, by Misseduc
  Foundation, Inc. Reprinted by the University Press of Mississippi 2017 by
  permission of Elisabeth Sifton and Hodding Carter III. Introduction
  copyright © University Press of Mississippi 2017"—ECIP title page. |
  Identifiers: LCCN 2017022083 (print) | LCCN 2017023715 (ebook) | ISBN
  9781496813442 (epub single) | ISBN 9781496813459 (epub institutional) |
  ISBN 9781496813466 (pdf single) | ISBN 9781496813473 (pdf institutional)
  | ISBN 9781496813428 (cloth : alk. paper) | ISBN 9781496813435 (pbk : alk.
  paper)
Subjects: LCSH: Police brutality—Mississippi. | Violence—Mississippi. |
  Police—Mississippi. | Law enforcement—Mississippi. | African
  Americans—Mississippi.
Classification: LCC HV8145.M7 (ebook) | LCC HV8145.M7 M57 2017 (print) | DDC
  323.1196/073076209046—dc23
LC record available at https://lccn.loc.gov/2017022083

British Library Cataloging-in-Publication Data available

Contents

Introduction to the New Edition VII
JASON MORGAN WARD

Publisher's Note XXIX

Foreword XXXI
REINHOLD NIEBUHR

Introduction XXXIII
HODDING CARTER III

Statements and Affidavits. 1

Index. 113

Introduction to the New Edition

IN EARLY FEBRUARY 1964, GREENE BREWER PULLED OVER AT A COUNTRY store in Tallahatchie County, Mississippi, to put air in a tire. Along with his younger brother Charles, who had moved to Indianapolis three years earlier, the twenty-nine-year-old New Jersey resident had returned home to visit family and friends. While Greene filled the tire, Charles went into Huntly's Grocery to buy some soft drinks. Hearing a commotion inside the store, Greene Brewer headed for the door. When he entered the store, he saw his brother bleeding and unconscious on the floor. As Brewer tried to drag his brother out of the store, a white man named George Little bludgeoned him with an axe handle. Despite suffering a fractured skull, cracked jawbone, broken nose, and burst eyeball, Greene Brewer somehow managed to load his brother into the car and drive off.[1]

After delivering his injured younger brothers to a local hospital, Percy Lee Brewer went to see a white attorney. "He said he wished he could help," the farmer later noted in a sworn affidavit, "but that it would be a 'knock' on him." As a member of the diehard segregationist Citizens' Council, the attorney wanted nothing to do with the "negro problem"—despite the fact that the Brewer brothers had no history of civil rights activism. The provocation for the attack, as Charles Brewer recounted after regaining consciousness, was his failure to "sir" the storeowner when he purchased his sodas. "When a damn nigger goes North and comes back," the proprietor spat, "he gets beside himself, and he gets where he can't respect white folk." A different version of the incident had reached the county sheriff, who was even less sympathetic to Percy Brewer's appeal on behalf of his hospitalized brothers. "They are lucky—they are supposed to be dead," Sheriff Ellett R. Dogan replied, "Because of them coming in cussing." Left with no alternative, and a $212 hospital bill, Percy Brewer headed north to Clarksdale to contact the NAACP.[2]

Four months after the attack, Greene and Percy Brewer traveled to the nation's capital with a busload of black Mississippians. On June 8, 1964, at a public hearing organized by allies of the Council of Federated Organizations

(COFO), the Brewers and their companions testified to the violence and harassment faced by civil rights workers and everyday people in a time of mounting racial hostility. Even as COFO launched its daring Summer Project, which by month's end would bring over a thousand college-aged volunteers into Mississippi, the "showcase hearing" at the National Theater reflected COFO's ongoing effort to document and publicize racial violence in the hopes of securing federal protection for civil rights workers and supporters. To that end, COFO and its allies collected scores of affidavits from seasoned activists, volunteers, and everyday people across Mississippi. If those efforts failed to compel federal protection, they provided the source base for the *Mississippi Black Paper*—a slim volume that stands apart from the deluge of memoirs and exposés published in the wake of Freedom Summer. While accounts by journalists, social scientists, and participant observers poured forth in the months and years following the Mississippi Summer Project, the *Black Paper* emphasized the testimony of a broad range of people to the conditions that prevailed in the Magnolia State during a period of intense conflict over the fate of Jim Crow.[3]

Unlike many of the black Mississippians who testified at the National Theater in June 1964, Greene Brewer's name does not appear in *Mississippi Black Paper*. Along with a handful of other individuals whose testimonies are published in the book, Brewer could not be reached for permission at the time of publication. Rather than omit powerful accounts from those who "had moved—presumably for obvious reasons," the publisher printed Brewer's story anonymously. The supporting statements from his family members, along with approximately two hundred additional affidavits collected by COFO and its allies, did not make the final list of fifty-seven testimonies included in the *Mississippi Black Paper*. Yet the broader effort to collect and document these accounts, distilled into book form in early 1965, reflects both the immediate strategic significance of racial violence in the development of the Mississippi civil rights movement and the historical importance of such testimony to the black freedom struggle. By bearing witness to white terrorism and abuse of power in Mississippi, Greene Brewer and dozens of others—many of whose names barely register in a survey of the existing literature on Mississippi's civil rights saga—defied the culture of silence and suppression that perpetuated Jim Crow. Their testimony did not dynamite the pillars of brutality, terror, complicity, and denial that propped up Mississippi's white supremacist regime, but collectively these accounts helped shape a national conversation on the fundamental violence of Mississippi's segregated social order.

Greene Brewer's name may have been lost to history, or at least overshadowed by the hundreds of black Mississippians written into the state's civil rights story, but his testimony highlights some of the important themes and questions raised in *Mississippi Black Paper*. First, the brutal attack he and his brother endured serves as a reminder that seemingly isolated incidents of racial violence could assume world-historical significance. In the same corner of the Mississippi Delta where an earlier encounter at a country store cash register sparked the most famous lynching in American history, the Brewers found themselves pulled into the civil rights struggle via white supremacists' volatile anxieties. Emmett Till would have been nearly the same age as Greene's younger brother Charles. Whites deemed both suspect on account of their time "up North," and neither victims' family could expect any semblance of justice in Tallahatchie County. Separated by nearly a decade, these two incidents of violence resulted in vastly different levels of publicity and notoriety. Yet they serve as a reminder that regardless of how little Tallahatchie County—and Mississippi—had changed between 1955 and 1964, local whites responded violently precisely because they understood the gathering threats to the racial status quo.

Indeed, despite the seemingly random nature of the attack on the Brewer brothers, anti-black violence had a logic and rationale that preceded Freedom Summer and persisted in its wake. While Freedom Summer and the violence it provoked feature prominently in *Mississippi Black Paper*, the testimony establishes a longer timeline of violence and intimidation that reached back to the mid-1950s. As the Brewers' experience reveals, that campaign of terror served to keep whites in line as well. The attorney who feared ostracism by fellow Citizens' Councilors, ostensibly more respectable and less violent than Klansmen, revealed how anti-civil rights harassment discouraged whites from challenging white supremacy. Repression took various forms, from social ostracism to economic coercion, but opposition to racial change fueled violence and allowed it to go unpunished. Yet in the Brewers' story, and in testimony throughout the book, snippets of evidence suggest that white racial orthodoxy was neither monolithic nor unchanging—even in the face of rampant violence.

The vicious assault on the Brewer brothers also highlights how acts of violence repeatedly compelled individuals, families, and communities to action. While local white supremacists deemed Percy Lee Brewer's "northern" brothers suspect, it was their local farmer brother who sought help from civil rights activists and FBI agents. And long after Greene and Charles returned home, their relatives became civil rights trailblazers. Just six months after the beating at Huntly's Grocery, which brought the Brewer family into COFO's orbit, four members of the Brewer family attempted to register to vote—the first attempt by blacks in Tallahatchie County since Reconstruction. A local voter registration project, one of thirty across the state staffed by COFO workers and Freedom Summer volunteers, provided legal support.[4]

Finally, the intermingling of well-known activists with the anonymous and obscure in the pages of *Mississippi Black Paper* reveals how much of the state's civil rights story remains untold. Mississippi has always loomed large in the historiography of the black freedom struggle, but even the most studied of states still offers much to explore. The inclusion of testimony from across the state, including counties that witnessed no organized activity during Freedom Summer, reveals the pervasiveness of white supremacist violence and harassment at the climactic moment of the Mississippi Movement. On the other hand, the inclusion of affidavits and statements from only a fraction of Mississippi's eighty-two counties underscores how much of the state remained off the movement's beaten path. Yet *Black Paper* was never intended to be comprehensive. As evidenced by its brevity, omissions, and errors, the book was meant for the moment.

Suspended between the two most pivotal summers of the civil rights era, that moment was highly volatile. Published in the months following the Summer Project, the passage of the 1964 Civil Rights Act, and the mobilization of the Mississippi Freedom Democratic Party, the *Black Paper* recounted a campaign of violence and terror that undercut triumphal "turning point" narratives and hopeful forecasts of better days ahead. The testimonies, which document anti-civil rights incidents through the end of July 1964, offered a collective call for action in a highly contingent moment. With no apparent end in sight, the brutality demanded a response. By compiling the *Mississippi Black Paper*, the latest in a series of opportunities for activists and everyday people to bear witness to the violence and terror they encountered, COFO and its allies hoped to fuel public pressure and compel federal intervention.

It was a tall order for a short book. While the precise origin story of *Black Paper* is difficult to reconstruct, civil rights groups in Mississippi had amassed enough testimonies to fill an encyclopedia. Since its inception, COFO poured a significant amount of time and resources into documenting incidents of violence and harassment. At COFO's Jackson office, civil rights workers monitored the Wide Area Telephone Service (WATS) line around the clock. The flat-rate, long-distance service—which allowed civil rights workers in rural areas to bypass local operators—facilitated a constant stream of incident reports. With assistance from local activists and attorneys, COFO collected scores of signed affidavits that elaborated on these incidents and provided legal documentation for suits and injunctions. In addition to litigation, the testimonies proved essential to COFO's information offensive. As SNCC veteran and COFO program director Bob Moses explained at the June 8, 1964 hearing at Washington's National Theater, testimonies of violence could "open to the country and the world some of the facts which we who work in Mississippi know only too well. . . . [but] which, for one reason or another, have not been publicly aired and it is very difficult to get across to the country." These stories of brutality and injustice, civil rights workers hoped, would shock the public conscience, spur congressional action, and compel federal protection of civil rights workers.[5]

Mississippi Black Paper resulted directly from this two-pronged strategy of legal action and public testimony. As the publisher's note acknowledges, COFO had collected the statements and affidavits to offer as evidence in a suit brought against Neshoba County sheriff Lawrence Rainey, whose alleged role in the deaths and disappearance of civil rights workers James Chaney, Andrew Goodman, and Michael Schwerner in June 1964 made him the most notorious lawman in Mississippi. Yet the sprawling collection of evidence reflected a far more ambitious goal. COFO brought suit against Rainey, as the publisher's note explains, "both as an individual and as a representative of similar public servants in all eighty-two counties of Mississippi." Indeed, the suit filed in US District Court named not only Rainey and his deputy Cecil Price, but also the Mississippi Highway Patrol, the Citizens' Councils, Ku Klux Klan, and the Americans for the Preservation of the White Race, and "others whose identity is presently to the plaintiffs unknown." After Judge Harold Cox, a staunch obstructionist of civil rights litigation, dismissed the suit without a hearing, COFO appealed for an injunction, as noted in the excerpt from the complaint filed in the Fifth Circuit of the US Court of Appeals, against the use of "force, violence or any terroristic act" by officials and private citizens.[6]

The precise moment when this legal maneuvering birthed a book is difficult to pinpoint, but by the end of 1964 COFO had established connections with influential northern liberals and legal aid organizations. Strengthened and broadened by the Summer Project and the Mississippi Freedom Democratic Party's historic challenge at the Democratic National Convention in Atlantic City, this network provided a path to prestigious publishers. The inclusion of a foreword by Reinhold Niebuhr, the foremost theologian of his generation and a major influence on Martin Luther King Jr. and other civil rights leaders, reflects the connections forged between the Mississippi Movement and progressive religious bastions like Union Theological Seminary—Niebuhr's home institution—and the National Council of Churches. The NCC, which sent three hundred clergy into Mississippi during Freedom Summer, later established its own long-term community development project, the Delta Ministry, in the state.[7]

Less obscure, and perhaps more revealing, than the book's path to publication is the selection and organization of the fifty-seven testimonies included. Chosen from a trove of 257 statements, as the publisher's note explains, "for the variety and cruelty of the harassment and brutality they describe," the affidavits documented a wide range of abuses. Indeed, COFO's legal team had organized the original collection of affidavits into six categories. The majority of the affidavits collected, 160 by COFO's count, documented various forms of police brutality, harassment, and dereliction of duty. Only a handful of statements documented another important failing of state officials— "the misuse of power by members of the Mississippi judiciary." The remaining statements recounted acts of physical violence, arson, and vandalism committed by private citizens against civil rights workers and supporters.

The evidence presented in *Mississippi Black Paper* hammers home the reality that no black Mississippian or suspect outsider was safe from violence and harassment. Nevertheless, the geographic distribution of the testimonies reflects the extent of organized civil rights activity at the height of Freedom Summer. The collection of 257 affidavits documented incidents in twenty-seven of Mississippi's eighty-two counties, largely concentrated in the Mississippi Delta, the state's southwestern corner, and larger cities and towns including Jackson, Meridian, Gulfport, Biloxi, Hattiesburg, Laurel, Vicksburg, Natchez, and Columbus. Most of these communities benefitted from at least one Summer Project initiative—voter registration drives, community center programs, Freedom Schools, or health clinics sponsored by the Medical Committee for Human Rights.

Incidents from sixteen of these original twenty-seven counties are included in *Mississippi Black Paper,* and the geographic distribution is more skewed. Northeast Mississippi, the Gulf Coast, and most of the state's southern and eastern counties are not represented. A belt of central Mississippi counties that witnessed significant civil rights activity, from Meridian in the east to Jackson and Vicksburg in the west, are featured at least once, yet south of that swath more than a dozen counties neither benefitted from those initiatives nor contributed documentation of the reprisals such programs provoked. COFO allies collected nearly thirty affidavits in neighboring Jones and Forrest counties, home to Laurel and Hattiesburg respectively. Yet in the rural counties surrounding these twin hubs of the Piney Woods region, COFO neither launched Freedom Summer projects nor collected any documentation of violence and harassment.

These geographic patterns are instructive. They reflect the predominance of the Student Nonviolent Coordinating Committee (SNCC) in the Mississippi Movement and the COFO coalition. The theater of operations assigned to the Congress of Racial Equality (CORE)—a congressional district that stretched from just north of Jackson to the state's eastern border—figures prominently in *Black Paper* due to the murders of Meridian-based civil rights workers in neighboring Neshoba County. Yet save for a handful of statements from Neshoba and Madison counties, activities in CORE's Fourth Congressional District barely factor into *Mississippi Black Paper.* For practical and historically specific reasons, the book places greater emphasis on hubs of organized civil rights activity. Yet, as the testimony from Neshoba County suggests, workers based in larger towns and cities frequently fanned out into surrounding counties previously untouched by movement activity. In Meridian, CORE's headquarters for the eastern half of the Fourth Congressional District, Schwerner and other staffers ventured not only into Neshoba County but also into other neighboring counties. As Schwerner's widow, Rita, later recalled, "There was good reason why Mickey wanted to do more in the outlying counties. . . . life was much harder for the Negroes, they had less to lose, so the adults were ready to take more risks."[8]

While civil rights activity—and anti-civil rights violence—extended beyond the counties mentioned in *Mississippi Black Paper*, particular areas of the state figure prominently for good reason. The geographic clusters of the affidavits attest to persistent activity, organizational presence, and recurrent violence in particular areas of the state, and testimonies from these beachheads fill more than their share of the book's pages. Proceeding in rough chronological order, the first several affidavits not only identify hubs of movement activity but also trace a longer timeline of activism and retaliation that foregrounds the apparent explosion of anti-civil rights violence during Freedom Summer.

The book's first testimony reflects the importance of grassroots leadership and earlier civil rights milestones to the emergence of the Mississippi Movement. E. W. Steptoe, a black landowner and dairy farmer, dated his own activism from 1954. The head of the NAACP branch in Amite County, in the rural southwestern corner of the state, Steptoe had recruited nearly two hundred members before the *Brown* decision sparked a local wave of repression. After the county sheriff disrupted a branch meeting and confiscated the membership list, as Steptoe recounts, he and his fellow members lived in perpetual fear of reprisals. With an active Klan presence, cross burnings, and reports of threats and attacks on neighbors, Steptoe wrote, "There is not an hour which passes when I do not feel my life is in danger." No one had paid a visit to his home, he noted, which likely had as much to do with his arsenal of firearms as with the fact that he lived "very far off the highway."

Steptoe's testimony highlights an aspect of civil rights activism that is largely absent from *Mississippi Black Paper*. Published at the height of a nonviolent mass movement, the book includes very few mentions of armed self-defense. In a notable exception, Ora Lee Bryant—sister-in-law of Pike County NAACP head C. C. Bryant—describes shooting at a passing carload of men as they tossed a bundle of dynamite towards her home. Such acts of armed resistance could not prevent the racial terrorism documented in *Mississippi Black Paper*, but the self-defense tradition proved as essential to the movement's survival in Mississippi as nonviolent direct action was to its political success. Despite his philosophical commitment to nonviolence, SNCC organizer Bob Moses sought out Steptoe and Bryant in 1961 when he initiated the organization's first voter registration project in Mississippi. In spite of the Southwest's reputation as a particularly violent corner of the state, it became a hotbed of SNCC activity.[9]

Nonviolent direct action developed in tandem and in tension with black Mississippians' tradition of armed self-defense. The same year that SNCC set up shop in the southwestern corner of the state, the Congress of Racial Equality (CORE) arrived in Mississippi via the Freedom Riders. After the interracial group of activists strode into Jackson's Trailways bus terminal and the waiting arms of local police, the capital city endured a wave of protest. Jesse Harris, one of the young Jacksonians pulled into the movement, dates his involvement in the movement and his encounter with police brutality and harassment from the 1961 Freedom Rides. Harris, along with dozens of black and white Freedom Riders, spent several weeks at the Mississippi State Penitentiary—a galvanizing experience that historian Raymond Arsenault has called "the first 'freedom summer'"—in addition to enduring beatings and solitary confinement in the Hinds County Jail's "sweatbox" the following year. The inclusion of his testimony, following that of an older grassroots activist, reflects the pivotal role of CORE's Freedom Rides in "cracking" the state and connecting with a younger generation of black Mississippians who would prove crucial to the success of later campaigns.[10]

After the first two statements, *Black Paper* shifts focus to the emergence of nonviolent direct action in the Mississippi Delta. Several testimonies from the counties of Coahoma and Leflore recount incidents of violence and harassment in 1962 and 1963. The passages underscore the strategic importance and organizing tradition of the black-majority Delta region. Clarksdale, county seat of Coahoma, was a site of longstanding civil rights activism. In 1958, three years before Martin Luther King Jr. traveled to Jackson in the wake of the Freedom Rides, the civil rights leader visited Clarksdale for a pivotal early gathering of his fledgling Southern Christian Leadership Conference (SCLC). The town was also an important NAACP hub, due in large part to local pharmacist Aaron Henry. Elected state NAACP president in 1960, Henry proved—in the words of historian John Dittmer— "the most ecumenical of Mississippi activists." As such, he spearheaded local protest campaigns in the early 1960s that attracted support from SNCC, SCLC, and CORE, paving the way for the eventual establishment of COFO.[11]

A notary public, Henry is also a primary reason that more than a quarter of the statements in *Mississippi Black Paper*—fifteen in all—come from Coahoma County. With the assistance of civil rights workers and legal aid groups, Henry started collecting and notarizing affidavits of harassment and abuse before COFO came into existence. The earliest of these testimonies document white backlash to an NAACP boycott launched in late 1961 and expanded in the following months to include a voter registration drive and demands for the desegregation of schools and public facilities. In Henry's statement, he describes the 1962 bombing of his home and drug store in retaliation for bringing Clarksdale's local struggle to national prominence. Additional statements by Clarksdale NAACP members, civil rights workers, and local youth document a vicious campaign of police brutality and harassment that proceeded unchecked through Freedom Summer.

In Greenwood, the seat of Leflore County, SNCC launched its most ambitious voter registration drive in 1962. Initially spearheaded by Sam Block, an unpaid twenty-three-year-old staffer from the Delta town of Cleveland, the Greenwood campaign became SNCC's largest initiative in the region by 1963. Block, one of only a few individuals to contribute two statements—both unattributed—to *Mississippi Black Paper*, describes intimidation and attacks by private citizens and hostile indifference from local police. Although he avoided serious injury when vigilantes fired into his car from a passing station wagon, his comrade Jimmy Travis, a twenty-year-old SNCC field secretary, suffered bullet wounds to the neck and shoulder in a similar attack.[12]

The violent backlash to civil rights activism targeted women as well as men. While only a dozen women's testimonies appear in *Mississippi Black Paper*, half of them appear in the first third of the book. The failure of the book's creators to include more women's testimonies is glaring, yet these accounts point to the foundational role of women in the Mississippi Movement. The first three, all from Coahoma County, attest to the dangers facing women caught up in Clarksdale's burgeoning civil rights campaigns. When Vera Mae Pigee reported a white service station attendant who beat her for asking to use the restroom, Clarksdale police charged the NAACP branch secretary with "disturbing the peace." Hattie Mae Gilmore, a fellow NAACP member, faced criminal charges and loss of employment after leading pickets outside a white church. The briefest, and most searing, testimony came from a younger woman, Bessie Turner, whom police detained in the early months of Clarksdale's boycott campaign. After arresting her for an alleged theft, police forced the twenty-one-year-old to take off her clothes before beating her across her thighs, pelvis, and breasts.

The gendered coercion and sexualized violence that women faced made their testimonies all the more powerful. Another trio of testimonies, from civil rights workers arrested and beaten in Winona in June 1963, attest to women's vulnerability to a particularly vicious brand of police brutality. Fannie Lou Hamer, arguably the most recognizable name in the collection, contributed the most widely recognizable story. The former Delta sharecropper had endured eviction, forced sterilization, harassment, and death threats since she attempted to register to vote in 1962. She recounted the story of her brutal beating in the Winona jail, which occurred on a trip home from a voter registration workshop in Charleston, South Carolina, throughout her life. Most notably, Hamer told the story in front of a nationally televised credentials committee hearing at the 1964 Democratic National Convention.

Unfortunately, Hamer's testimony, the most infamous in *Black Paper*, is also the most glaring error in the original text. Perhaps a consequence of the haste with which the book was published, the final ten paragraphs of Hamer's affidavit appeared on pages 21 and 22 as part of Annell Ponder's testimony. As this edition preserves the text as originally published, the misattributed text remains here. Yet the combined impact of Hamer, Ponder, and sixteen-year-old June Johnson's accounts, printed in succession, foregrounded the triumph and tragedy of the following summer in a longstanding history of gendered violence and terror. Lorne Cress, a black Chicagoan who participated in the Summer Project in Forrest County, testifies to the sexual humiliation she faced when local police pulled over a car carrying her and five white male volunteers in July 1964. After accusing Cress of riding around "with your dress over your head" and having sex with all five men in the car, he threatened the men and added, "I hope niggers are raping your mothers."[13]

Increasingly, historians have acknowledged the extent of women's activism in the face of sexually charged violence and harassment. *Black Paper* does not shy away from these taboos, but women's testimony nearly as often emphasizes their roles as witnesses to violence. This limitation speaks to gendered assumptions that prevailed among allies of the civil rights movement as well as its opponents. Tellingly, the two longest passages in *Black Paper* come from widows. Michael Schwerner's wife Rita, who continued to work for COFO in Jackson and Greenwood while authorities searched for her husband and his colleagues, recounted the months of mounting intimidation that led up to their disappearance and the callous indifference of officials afterwards. Elizabeth Allen's statement describes the harassment her husband Lewis faced after he challenged white officials' account of the 1961 killing of Amite County civil rights leader Herbert Lee. In early 1964, unidentified assailants shot Lewis Allen dead.

The power of women's testimonies in *Mississippi Black Paper* notwithstanding, the relatively low number of them distorts our view of the movement. That a third of these statements came from Clarksdale, a site of sustained activism and leadership by women, suggests a more prominent place in the civil rights saga than *Black Paper* reflects. Despite their lack of visibility in this book, women's influence and visibility in the movement—and their place in its history—would only increase from 1964 onward. With the emergence of grassroots antipoverty and educational initiatives, from the formation of economic cooperatives to the pioneering Child Development Group of Mississippi and other Head Start agencies, women's role in fostering racial change is increasingly central to the state's civil rights story.[14]

For all that it may reveal about the Mississippi Movement's foundations and forerunners, *Black Paper* is above all a product of Freedom Summer. From the influx of northern volunteers to the mass mobilization campaign launched by the MFDP, the "long, hot summer" elevated the state's civil rights struggle to national prominence. Surprisingly, relatively few of the testimonials included come from northern volunteers, and their statements only describe incidents through the final weeks of July. Given that the preparations for the MFDP's historic challenge at the Democratic National Convention did not ramp up until late July, and that the bodies of Chaney, Goodman, and Schwerner lay undiscovered in a earthen dam until early August, *Mississippi Black Paper* provides an unfinished portrait of a pivotal moment. As a result, the testimonies chart a widening and worsening white backlash, with civil rights workers, black Mississippians, and suspect outsiders caught in the turmoil.

Northern volunteers and supporters testify to widespread police violence and vigilante activity across the state. David Riley, a "research man" for the summer project in Warren County, documents the burning of a black community center in the rural community of Bovina and officials' role in the disappearance of the three-foot torch that sparked the blaze. Testimony from a Connecticut minister and a New York rabbi, both of whom faced harassment and threats from police and local whites, underscore the importance of the hundreds of clergy who came to Mississippi during Freedom Summer. Certainly, these volunteers and supporters faced more than threats, as evidenced by Michigan native Peter Werner's beating in front of a Hattiesburg drug store. After a white man bloodied the summer volunteer, local police arrested Werner for assault and battery.

The accounts from Werner and other volunteers in Forrest and neighboring Jones county, the heart of southern Mississippi's Piney Woods region, comprise the most significant cluster of testimony from the state's eastern half. COFO gathered the bulk of these affidavits at the height of Freedom Summer, and the accounts highlight the connection between national civil rights politics and grassroots activity in Mississippi. In Laurel, attempts to "test" the recently passed Civil Rights Act resulted in beatings and arrests at cafes and department store lunch counters. The headquarters of the Mississippi White Knights of the Ku Klux Klan, a notoriously violent faction implicated in the Neshoba murders, Laurel also witnessed vigilante intimidation of local civil rights leaders. "If you don't want the same thing to happen to you that happened to the three civil rights workers in Neshoba County," read a note wrapped around a rock chucked through the window of an office shared by a black physician and dentist, "stop working with the NAACP."[15]

White resentment of the Summer Project also led to harassment and abuse of black Mississippians with no clear connection to the movement. In Clarksdale, police detained fifty-eight-year-old Joe Johnson for allegedly scratching a white woman's car, and then beat him for *looking* at their female office clerk. "Don't look a white lady in the face, you goddamn son of a bitch," growled the attacking officer. In the only statement from Sharkey County, A.C. Whitaker—unidentified in the original edition—endured a savage beating by a highway patrolman when he returned to inquire about his car, which he had left parked on the side of the highway after a wheel hub came loose. The forty-year-old father of nine, who worked as a heavy equipment mechanic at a NASA test site on the Gulf Coast, passed through the south Delta county frequently on his drives home to Greenville. But any outsider—white or black—was suspect during Freedom Summer. "Go back to Greenville," the patrolman barked, "and tell all the niggers in Greenville that they beat a nigger's ass in Sharkey County."[16]

Black Paper provides searing glimpses into the racial climate of Freedom Summer. Indeed, while fewer than half of the book's entries describe incidents that occurred during the Summer Project, the book's framing and reception privilege this immediate historical context. Reinhold Niebuhr's foreword captures succinctly both the Mississippi Movement's moral witness and its pragmatic engagement with the mechanisms of American government. The prominent theologian, a pivotal influence not only on Martin Luther King Jr. but also on the scores of clergy who descended on Mississippi and other southern states at the height of the civil rights movement, argues that the *Black Paper* testimonies proved "the absolute necessity of the Civil Rights Bill for the sake of this country's political health." Niebuhr balances a healthy disgust for Mississippi's "closed society"—a phrase borrowed from the title of University of Mississippi history professor James Silver's 1964 indictment of the state's political climate—with an acknowledgment of the nation's longstanding failure to secure racial justice. In language reflecting COFO's own characterization of Mississippi's Jim Crow status quo, Niebuhr argues that "crimes of arbitrary justice have claimed their Negro victims for decades—ever since the victorious Union allowed the former slave states to preserve vestiges of slavery." With comparisons to Nazi Germany and South Africa, the author of the 1932 classic *Moral Man and Immoral Society* argued that only "national standards of justice" could redeem "a society in which the instruments of justice are tools of injustice."[17]

Hodding Carter III makes no reference to Niebuhr's foreword in his lengthier introduction, but the theologian might well have concurred with the white Mississippian's assertion that the backlash against Freedom Summer "was not the result of some extraordinary historical accident which found a vast assemblage of evil men in the wrong place at the wrong time." Anticipating white Mississippians' attempts to deny or dispute the book's contents, Carter defends the collection as "a truthful presentation." Pushing back against the notion of a closed society, the son of Pulitzer Prize-winning Greenville newspaperman and racial moderate Hodding Carter II, placed the blame on "the silence of good men" and the "system" that demanded "public toleration of the excesses of the vicious and ignorant." The similarities between Carter and Niebuhr largely end there, as the Mississippi journalist frames the summer's eruption of violence as a turning point in the state's racial politics. In a departure from the foreboding tone and progression of the testimonials that follow, Carter offers a eulogy of sorts for a terror campaign that had run its course and awakened white Mississippians of goodwill to their civic duty, or at least convinced them of the futility and immorality of violent resistance.[18]

The decision to invite Carter to pen the book's introduction attests to the newspaperman's credibility in the northern liberal network that ushered *Mississippi Black Paper* to publication. Carter had barely graduated from Princeton when he chronicled the rise of the Citizens' Council in 1959's *The South Strikes Back,* and by the early 1960s he had taken his father's place as editor of the *Delta Democrat-Times*. Carter also spearheaded a progressive faction committed to building an interracial coalition within the state Democratic Party that could wrest control from the white supremacist Regulars. Carter cultivated close ties with state NAACP leaders like Aaron Henry, but many civil rights workers remained aloof from what they perceived as a middle-class, moderate alternative to the MFDP. By the time Carter penned his introduction, he had emerged as an influential but polarizing figure in civil rights politics.

In his characterization of civil rights workers and summer volunteers, Carter provides a glimpse of the fault lines in COFO's united front. He portrays the northern volunteers as "a varied lot," with jabs at "utopians," "oddballs," and "extreme Leftists," but concedes that the volunteers' sincerity ultimately outweighed their naiveté and "distorted radicalism." If the Summer Project lacked in concrete gains, the volunteers had "dispelled most Mississippi Negroes' well-founded belief that the rest of the country did not care what happened to them." As for the various constituent elements of the COFO coalition, Carter characterizes SNCC veterans as "battle-hardened and sometimes bitterly cynical," CORE as limited and largely inconsequential, and "black racists" as betrayers of the Project's integrationist goals. Carter notes that COFO and its allies had not closed up shop with the departure of the summer volunteers, but quickly adds that the NAACP "is publicly airing its displeasure at some of the organization's tactics."

Writing in April 1965, eight months after the MFDP delegation's unsuccessful attempt to claim the seats of Mississippi's all-white Regulars at the Democratic National Convention, Carter anticipates COFO's demise from the perspective of someone with a decided interest in the outcome. As a chief architect of an emerging interracial coalition within the Mississippi Democratic Party, Carter portrays the MFDP's Atlantic City challenge as a long-term victory that would pave the way for his own faction—the NAACP-backed Loyal Democrats. He attributes the "triumph" in part to the "political death-wish" of the segregationist Regulars, whom the Loyal delegation would successfully replace at the 1968 Democratic Convention. What Carter fails to acknowledge, and likely knew by early 1965, was that MFDP was soldiering on as an independent political organization that enjoyed widespread grassroots support. The MFDP's 1965 Congressional Challenge, an attempt to contest the seating of the state's five congressmen and force a new election, mobilized thousands but also alienated the NAACP and white liberal allies.

The COFO-backed campaign also tested Carter's prediction that police brutality and racial terrorism would decline. In June 1965, Jackson police packed hundreds of black Mississippians and a fresh batch of summer volunteers into state fairground cattle pens after they marched on the capitol to protest the legislature's attempts to undermine the Congressional Challenge and circumvent the new Voting Rights Act.[19]

Carter predicts the impending return of summer volunteers in 1965, and pivotal events during and since Mississippi's "summer of shame" predetermined their experience. The passage of the Voting Rights Act, and the threat of federal registrars taking over local officials' voter rolls, paved the way for a massive registration drive. Volunteers ventured into new counties and communities, and new federally-funded Head Start programs operated alongside adult literacy programs and health clinics. In communities largely untouched by the previous summer's campaign, civil rights workers and local blacks continued to "test" the provisions of the Civil Rights Act at local eateries, theaters, and public facilities. Carter's prediction that "the intensity of the pattern of last summer will not be duplicated" proved prescient, although officials and local whites continued to harass and attack civil rights workers and their supporters.[20]

As plans for another summer campaign ramped up, Random House published *Mississippi Black Paper*. Like Carter's introduction, reviewers framed the book as a retrospective on the previous summer's brutality. One of many "Mississippi books" published in the wake of Freedom Summer, *Black Paper* stood out as a singular contribution. Walker Percy, a National Book Award-winning author who, like Carter, was raised in Greenville, penned a feature review essay in a July issue of the *New York Review of Books*. Alongside half a dozen other recent books in a rapidly expanding subgenre, including Sally Belfrage's *Freedom Summer*; Elizabeth Sunderland's *Letters from Mississippi*; William McCord's *Mississippi: The Long Hot Summer*; and William Bradford Huie's *Three Lives for Mississippi*, the novelist echoed Carter's conclusion that "the indictment of Mississippi is already in." Likewise, Percy declared the situation much improved a year later. Bemoaning the "sameness" of violence and white terrorists' lack of "imagination," Percy saw little new or shocking in the stack of books before him. He declared the testimony in *Mississippi Black Paper*—the only book in the pile that prioritized and elevated black voices— "the most artless and terrible of all." He quoted from Bessie Turner and Vera Mae Pigee's accounts of beatings in Clarksdale, and conceded that there was "not much to say" in the face of such stark inhumanity.²¹

Black reviewers had plenty to say. "The power of this big paperback," *Ebony* announced, "derives from its simplicity." The black monthly blasted Random House, contrasting the bravery of those who contributed signed testimonies with a publisher that refused to print Mississippi police officers' names for fear of libel suits. In a *New York Times* review that featured *Black Paper* and eight other recent books dealing with race and civil rights, black scholar Saunders Redding expressed faith that "the American brand of human idealism" would overcome violence and bigotry. The prediction clashed not only with Niebuhr's theology of societal immorality, but also with Redding's earlier reaction in the pages of the Baltimore *Afro-American*. In a scathing review of *Black Paper,* nearly half of which quoted verbatim from Fannie Lou Hamer's account of her beating in Winona, Redding concluded that the fifty-seven statements "testify to a hatred so ingrained, so willful, so horrendous that even the blood of the Lamb cannot wash it away." In a similarly bleak vein, baseball great Jackie Robinson's syndicated column—bearing his imprint despite being guest-written by the head of the Associated Negro Press International—blasted the "palefaced storm troopers" and "white devils" responsible for the brutality. Echoing Niebuhr's allusions to other notorious racial regimes, the column concluded, "You feel as though maybe South Africa isn't such a bad place and perhaps Hitler was a kind man."²²

Mississippi officials likely brushed aside such rhetoric from the black press, but allusions to Nazi Germany by white journalists and public intellectuals clearly rankled those tasked with policing the state's public image. The Mississippi State Sovereignty Commission, a taxpayer-funded spy agency that kept tabs on perceived threats to segregation and operated as a public relations firm for Jim Crow, took exception to criticism fueled by *Black Paper* and other post-Freedom Summer exposés. When *Chicago Tribune* columnist Robert Cromie echoed Niebuhr's allusions to Nazism— "Few things in Hitler's Germany were more openly done than many of the criminal acts cited here"—the Sovereignty Commission flagged both Niebuhr and Cromie, and filed away the column in its "publicity" files.²³

Reviewers and readers situated *Mississippi Black Paper* in the immediate political and historical moment, yet the book reflects a longer tradition of testimony in the black freedom struggle. In this deeper context, exposure mattered more than literary accolades. Beginning with the narratives of formally enslaved African Americans in the antebellum era, black people bore witness to the violence and abuse they endured. Their testimony pricked the public conscience and fueled some of the most pivotal reform campaigns in American history. As historian Kidada Williams masterfully demonstrates in her study of black testimony from the Reconstruction era through the rise of Jim Crow, personal accounts of racial violence defied white supremacy and provided an evidentiary base for early civil rights campaigns. From black southerners who testified in Reconstruction-era congressional hearings to those who funneled eyewitness accounts of lynchings to the NAACP, their stories brought to life the statistical tallies and partisan scholarship of their allies and advocates.[24]

Black testimony bore witness to the web of state-sanctioned abuses, vigilante terrorism, and community complicity that fueled the culture of racial violence. Police brutality, rather than a response to black protest, was as essential to the maintenance of white supremacy as vigilante violence. Indeed, the book's subtitle emphasizes not extralegal extremism, but rather "police brutality, the breakdown of law and order and the corruption of justice"—all of which are presumably within the power of Mississippi officials to curtail. And while civil rights historians regularly cite *Mississippi Black Paper* as evidence of violence in a particular community or of the abuses endured by particular individuals, these anecdotes provide only a glimpse of the book's collective power and enduring message.

In an era of growing protests against police abuses and demands for reform, *Mississippi Black Paper* lives on. In September 2012, activists rallied at New York City Hall to demand an end to "stop-and-frisk" police tactics. The controversial and racially discriminatory practice, which peaked at approximately 685,000 stops in 2011, failed to lower robbery and burglary rates even as it sparked a vigorous protest campaign. At a City Hall rally the following year, speakers likened stop-and-frisk to "a new form of Jim Crow." As he spoke, Afro-Latino pastor Samuel Cruz waved an original copy of *Mississippi Black Paper*, with its blood-spattered cover, before the gathered crowd. The scene suggests that a book published as an indictment of police brutality in 1960s Mississippi still echoes in America's unfinished reckoning with race, violence, and history.[25]

JASON MORGAN WARD

NOTES

1. In addition to his testimony—printed without attribution—in *Mississippi Black Paper*, Greene Brewer's signed affidavit is filed with those of his two brothers and mother in the collection that forms the source base for the book. See Greene Brewer, signed affidavit, 24 May 1964, Box 3, Folder 22, Council of Federated Organizations Records, Call No. Z1867, Mississippi Department of Archives and History, Jackson (cited hereafter as COFO, MDAH).

2. Percy Lee Brewer, signed affidavit, 24 May 1964, Box 3, Folder 22, COFO, MDAH; Congress, House, 88th Cong., 2nd sess., *Congressional Record* 110, 13859.

3. Transcripts of the July 8, 1964, hearings at the National Theater were read into the Congressional Record the following week by sympathetic congressmen. For further discussion of the hearings, see Howard Zinn, *SNCC: The New Abolitionists* (c. 1964; Cambridge, MA: South End Press, 2002), 242–3; Carol Polsgrove, *Divided Minds: Intellectuals and the Civil Rights Movement* (New York: Norton, 2001), 227–231. The estimate of over one thousand Freedom Summer volunteers comes from the data compiled and evaluated by Doug McAdam, *Freedom Summer* (New York: Oxford, 1988), 4.

4. Council of Federated Organizations, "Affidavit I: Tallahatchie County," 2–3, box 5, folder 5, Susan Nichols Collection, Department of Special Collections and Archives, Queens College, New York, New York; *Voting in Mississippi: A Report of the United States Civil Rights Commission* (Washington, D.C.: GPO, 1965): 25.

5. Moses quoted in Chana Kai Lee, *For Freedom's Sake: The Life of Fannie Lou Hamer* (Urbana: University of Illinois Press, 2000), 78.

6. For a draft of the initial suit filed in US District Court, Southern District of Mississippi, see box 8, folder 22, Arthur Kinoy Papers, M20007-010, Wisconsin Historical Society, Madison, Wisconsin.

7. John Dittmer, *Local People: The Struggle for Civil Rights in Mississippi* (Urbana: University of Illinois Press, 1994), 336; Mark Newman, *Divine Agitators: The Delta Ministry and Civil Rights in Mississippi* (Athens: University of Georgia Press, 2004), 22.

8. William Bradford Huie, *Three Lives for Mississippi* (c. 1965; Jackson: University Press of Mississippi, 2000), 73–4.

9. The importance of Steptoe and the Bryants to the Mississippi Movement, and their reputation for armed self-defense, are profiled in Charles M. Payne, *I've Got the Light of Freedom: The Organizing Tradition and the Mississippi Freedom Struggle* (Berkeley: University of California Press, 1995), 111–114; Akinyele Omowale Umoja, *We Will Shoot Back: Armed Resistance in the Mississippi Freedom Movement* (New York: New York University Press, 2013), 59–63; Charles E. Cobb, *This Nonviolent Stuff'll Get You Killed: How Guns Made the Civil Rights Movement Possible* (New York: Basic Books, 2013), 143–44. For a recent cautionary analysis of the growing emphasis on

armed self-defense in civil rights historiography, see Emilye Crosby, "'It Wasn't the Wild West': Keeping Local Studies in Self-Defense Historiography," in Crosby, ed., *Civil Rights History From the Ground Up: Local Struggles, A National Movement* (Athens: University of Georgia Press, 2011), 194.

10. Raymond Arsenault, *Freedom Riders: 1961 and the Struggle for Racial Justice* (New York: Oxford University Press, 2006), 361, 481, 546.

11. Francoise N. Hamlin, *Crossroads at Clarksdale: The Black Freedom Struggle in the Mississippi Delta after World War II* (Chapel Hill: University of North Carolina Press, 2012), 54; Dittmer, *Local People*, 121–22; Minion K.C. Morrison, *Aaron Henry of Mississippi: Inside Agitator* (Fayetteville: University of Arkansas Press, 2015), 78.

12. Block's two signed—but not notarized—affidavits, printed anonymously on pages 9–10 and 12–13 of *Mississippi Black Paper*, are located in box 3, folder 12, COFO, MDAH.

13. In a subsequent publication of the testimonies of Hamer, Johnson, and Ponder, reprinted in an anthology of civil rights journalism, the editors acknowledged and corrected the error in *Mississippi Black Paper*. See Clayborne Carson, et al, eds. *Reporting Civil Rights, Part One: American Journalism, 1941–1963* (Library of America, 2003), 836–842, 951. On sexualized violence and the Winona jail beatings, see Lee, *For Freedom's Sake*, 58–59; Danielle McGuire, *At the Dark End of the Street: Black Women, Rape, and Resistance—A New History of the Civil Rights Movement from Rosa Parks to the Rise of Black Power* (New York: Knopf, 2010), 191–195.

14. Crystal R. Sanders, *A Chance for Change: Head Start and Mississippi's Black Freedom Struggle* (Chapel Hill: University of North Carolina Press, 2016); Hamlin, *Crossroads at Clarksdale*; Faith S. Holsaert, et al, eds, *Hands on the Freedom Plow: Personal Accounts by Women in SNCC* (Urbana: University of Illinois Press, 2010).

15. Patricia Michelle Boyett, *Right to Revolt: The Crusade for Racial Justice in Mississippi's Central Piney Woods* (Jackson: University Press of Mississippi, 2015).

16. A.C. Whitaker, handwritten affidavit, 26 July 1964, box 3, folder 20, COFO, MDAH.

17. James W. Silver, *Mississippi: The Closed Society* (New York: Harcourt, 1964).

18. Joseph Crespino, *In Search of Another Country: Mississippi and the Conservative Counterrevolution* (Princeton, NJ: Princeton University Press, 2007), 108–172.

19. Chris Danielson, *After Freedom Summer: How Race Realigned Mississippi Politics, 1965–1986* (Gainesville: University Press of Florida, 2011), 42; Dittmer, *Local People*, 338–353.

20. While the 1965 summer volunteers have received relatively little attention in scholarship on the Mississippi Movement, ample evidence of their activities is documented in the Project South interviews housed at the Stanford University Archives. Projects in Clay and Clarke counties, neither of which was included in the 1964 Summer Project, are featured in this collection, as well as expanded projects in

counties with pre-existing summer projects. Tellingly, the sponsoring agency for the 1965 summer programs is listed as MFDP, not COFO.

21. Walker Percy, "The Fire This Time," *New York Review of Books* 4:10 (1 July 1965): 3–5.

22. "Ebony Book Shelf," *Ebony* (September 1965): 22; Saunders Redding, "The South and Society," *New York Times,* 31 October 1965, 88–89; Saunders Redding, "Take Off Your Clothes," Baltimore *Afro-American,* 4 September 1965, A2; "Jackie Robinson Says: Miserable Mississippi," *Chicago Defender,* 24 July 1965, 10; "Jackie Robinson Says: Mississippi Is A Disgrace to Mankind," *Pittsburgh Courier,* 24 July 1965, 10.

23. Robert Cromie, "Affidavits of Cruelly in Mississippi Aired," *Chicago* Tribune, 27 July 1965, A2; clipping filed SCR ID# 6-54-0-96-1-1-1, Mississippi State Sovereignty Commission Records, MDAH.

24. Francis Smith Foster, *Witnessing Slavery: The Development of Antebellum Slave Narratives* (Madison: University of Wisonsin Press, 1979); Kidada E. Williams, *They Left Great Marks on Me: African American Testimonies of Racial Violence from Emancipation to World War I* (New York: NYU Press, 2012).

25. Karen Juanita Carrillo, "Rally Called to Reform Stop-and-Frisk," *New York Amsterdam News,* 3 October 2012, 3.

Publisher's Note

THESE AFFIDAVITS AND STATEMENTS WERE COLLECTED BY THE COUNCIL of Federated Organizations for the purpose of offering them in evidence in a suit brought against Sheriff Rainey—both as an individual and as a representative of similar public servants in all eighty-two counties of Mississippi—and other state officials. The purpose of the suit is to obtain the appointment of special federal commissioners to prevent violence against Negro citizens and civil rights workers in that state. The federal judge in Mississippi before whom the suit was brought dismissed it without a hearing, but the United States Court of Appeals for the Fifth Circuit reversed his decision and a hearing will soon be scheduled.

The fifty-seven testimonies on the following pages were chosen from a total of approximately 257 for the variety and cruelty of the harassment and brutality they describe. Before printing them the publishers secured the written permission of each of the victims; since many of these people still live in Mississippi, and therefore are subject to possible future hostility, we would like to thank them for their courage and cooperation.

Unfortunately, a few of the authors could not be traced by the time we went to press, because they had moved—presumably for obvious reasons—from their previous addresses; rather than omit these affidavits we have chosen to print them anonymously.

Lastly, an explanation is required for the large role played by "Officer A_____" (secondary parts being played, in progressively smaller roles, by "Officers B_____, C_____, D_____, E_____" and occasionally "F_____" and "G_____") in the following pages. Each of these alphabetized members of the cast, a police officer—often the sheriff or police chief—of the town in which the incident described took place, has been protected from specific identification only because of the high cost of defending libel suits in Mississippi. The publishers of these documents are convinced that eventually, on appeal outside the state, they would win whatever actions could be brought against them if the full names of the officials involved were printed. But the legal cost of scores of such suits, even when victory was achieved, would be enormous, and therefore we have reluctantly, on the advice of our lawyers, resorted to pseudonyms.

APRIL, 1965

Foreword

THIS COLLECTION OF NOTARIZED AFFIDAVITS AND STATEMENTS, GATHered by the Council of Federated Organizations—an association concerned, among its other goals, with helping Mississippi Negroes register to vote—gives eloquent testimony to the horrendous conditions of justice in a state that lacks both democratic disciplines and an independent judicial system. Yet this state is part of a nation which prides itself on having attained these two forms of political justice.

The documents disclose a society in which the instruments of justice are tools of *in*justice. On the evidence of these affidavits, it seems that there are no limits to inhumanity, cruelty and sheer caprice in a closed society, once social and communal restraints are no longer in force. The crimes described in the following pages, committed either by local officials or with their connivance, include the bombings of homes and churches, the arrests of Negroes on false charges for every type of fanciful law infraction, and—most frightening of all—a brutality by the police that frequently approaches sadistic cruelty and on occasion has resulted in actual murder.

The murder of the three freedom workers, after their arrest and detainment on a charge of speeding, is more understandable in light of the picture of legalized injustice these affidavits present. The affidavits also help to explain why the alleged murderer of the Negro civil rights leader, Medgar Evers, is still unpunished after several jury trials. The jury trial, in theory the final guarantee of justice, is in fact the criminal's final source of immunity in a corrupt society.

It is relevant to ask how these frightful standards of legalized injustice could have persisted for so long in a state which ostensibly is integral to the American community and shares its principle of democratic justice. Last summer the existing corruption of law and order in Mississippi was accentuated by the white oligarchy's knowledge that the registration of Negroes portended the end of its arbitrary rule. But crimes of arbitrary justice have claimed their Negro victims for decades—ever since the victorious Union allowed the former slave states to preserve vestiges of the slavery which the Civil War had supposedly abolished.

These documents will serve two purposes. On the moral level they reveal to the reader an important fact about human nature: that social discipline is the chief source of our much praised political humanity, so that in a community in which that discipline has been corrupted—in Nazi Germany, South Africa and some of the most benighted Southern states—cruelty and inhumanity flourish. But these affidavits also serve a more pragmatic purpose: they offer proof, if that is still needed, of the absolute necessity of the Civil Rights Bill for the sake of this country's political health.

The Civil Rights Bill was an expression of the national will and of national standards of justice, a resounding retort to the inhuman customs of local communities. On the evidence of the contents of this book, Mississippi standards can sink so low that only the legal and moral pressure of the larger community can redeem them—just as only the pressure of the British Commonwealth can save Northern Rhodesia from becoming another South Africa.

Not all the states of the Southern Confederacy have sunk to the standard of inhumanity described in these documents. Those that have not, have been more consciously and intimately a part of the national community and, therefore, subject to its economic, cultural and moral influences. Admittedly the national community has its own problems of racial prejudice and injustice, but the majesty of the law in the United States as a whole is preserved in no small part by the recognition by state and local communities that the federal government is the final source of law and order.

There are no quick or simple ways to eliminate the monstrous injustices revealed in these pages, but perhaps these affidavits will suggest to their readers that justice in Mississippi is corrupted to such a degree that without aid from the outside it is doomed.

REINHOLD NIEBUHR

Introduction

WHAT CAN A WHITE MISSISSIPPIAN SAY IN THE FACE OF THESE AFFIDAVITS? He can point out some of the possible exaggerations, cry foul because the allegations are presented with no attempt to balance them with rebuttals, or he can claim the incidents cited were exceptions rather than the general rule in Mississippi last year. He can point to such communities as my home town of Greenville which never experienced such events.

But though he can make at least a passable case for any of these objections, each of us in Mississippi knows in our heart that this is not enough. The truth is that the events recounted in this book are a truthful presentation of what too often occurred during the intensive civil rights activity in the state during the summer of 1964—whether all the charges in the following pages are completely correct or not. The shocking violations of simple justice and decency in some parts of Mississippi are a matter of well-documented public record. The message implicit in the murders of three civil rights workers in Neshoba County registers on our consciences despite all our equivocations and rationalizations.

What happened in my state last summer was not the result of some extraordinary historical accident which found a vast assemblage of evil men in the wrong place at the wrong time. Mississippi has no more than its share of bad or twisted individuals. The FBI's records indicate that, on the whole, Mississippi is one of the most crime-free states in the nation. The brutality, the bombings, the terror and the murders which dogged the integrationists' work can be accurately attributed to the silence of good men, bound by a system which in the name of self-preservation dictated public toleration of the excesses of the vicious and the ignorant.

The system had been almost inviolate since the end of Reconstruction. It was certainly little changed prior to last summer, despite the two previous national civil rights acts and the bloody occupation of the University of Mississippi to enforce its desegregation in 1962. Segregation was unquestioned publicly by all but a few whites, and the use of almost any device at hand to preserve "our way of life" was sanctioned by most businessmen as well as rednecks. Only a tiny group of isolated men and women, including a few editors, teachers and ministers, took open issue with the system and its results.

Upon this background was superimposed the Mississippi Summer Project, which was heralded with blaring publicity and projected as the modern equivalent of Jericho's trumpet. Few walls fell immediately, while what befell many of those who participated in the Project assumed a more immediate importance than its announced goals.

It is appalling, but true, that the most tangible outcome of the Summer Project is often measured by the murders in Neshoba County, by the destruction of almost forty Negro churches and by the beatings and arrests of hundreds of summer workers. When the raw statistics of that "long hot summer" are studied, there are few which can be easily placed on the asset side of the ledger by the Project's sponsor, the loose confederation of civil rights organizations which went under the title of Council of Federated Organizations (COFO). Some of its spokesmen claim a few score Negroes were registered here or attempted to register there, but most of these claims are educated guesses at best, and propaganda at worst. The summer's work made a heavy impact on the Negro community, but it did not pay off in substantial quantitative gains at the polls or on the employment rolls. The figures which can be produced are used to substantiate an indictment of white Mississippi, not to prove that COFO's volunteers scored a dramatic triumph in this regard.

The young men and women who came to Mississippi last summer and whose affidavits are the substance of this book were a varied lot. Most of them appeared to be sincere youngsters, sometimes a little naïve, who felt they were rendering a lasting service to the Negroes of Mississippi, to the cause of racial justice and to their nation. Their energy was infrequently matched by immediate and tangible results; their enthusiasm was too often unchanneled by intelligent organization. Nevertheless, the effect they had on the state's Negroes and its troubled whites will last longer than the rubble of the burned-out churches or the resurgence of the Ku Klux Klan, an ominous development which was antecedent to the Summer Project but directly related to the advance build-up given the "invasion."

There were others in COFO. Some were the battle-hardened and sometimes bitterly cynical veterans among the young professionals of the Student Nonviolent Coordinating Committee (SNCC). This organization provided most of the leadership for the local projects. There were some veterans from the Congress of Racial Equality (CORE), though there were far fewer of these and they were concentrated in certain sections of the state. There were also young utopians spouting a distorted radicalism they rarely understood but defiantly proclaimed; black racists who were sometimes openly contemptuous of their white co-workers and all other whites as well; and a small assortment of oddballs who defied categorization. The National Council of Churches lent guidance and counseling through some of its ministers, who for the most part did their best to channel COFO's work into constructive avenues.

Finally, there was the inevitable handful of extreme leftists and perhaps Communists, who attached themselves to the potentially revolutionary situation. Their material floated in and around the loosely controlled Project, as almost all newspapermen covering the scene knew. COFO frankly did little to screen this handful, and many of its spokesmen candidly admitted they were willing to take help from any source, with no questions asked. The great task in Mississippi precluded any "red baiting"—or so went the usual line.

From this wide assortment of Americans, plus a handful of curious foreigners, several positive effects were produced. First, the Project finally dispelled most Mississippi Negroes' well-founded belief that the rest of the country did not care what happened to them. The volunteers demonstrated that white men and women, as well as Negroes, were willing to live in the same deprived, squalid conditions and share the same dangers for the sake of local Negroes' "freedom," a much-repeated word which some Negroes could only vaguely define on a philosophical level but which few did not deeply desire.

The spark kindled by COFO did not flame high for all of Mississippi's Negroes, particularly those who were frightened or dulled by an apathy produced by the centuries-old awareness of the penalty for Negroes who did not keep their place. A small glow of appreciation is undoubtedly all that was produced in many of the older Negroes, for these are the permanent victims of a system which, throughout their lives, has denied them basic constitutional rights and any more than substandard education and employment. But COFO definitely made a significant impact on the younger Negro adults and those still in high school and college, who could realize that the 1964 Civil Rights Act was speaking directly to their condition.

From COFO's work came the first real stirrings of awareness that united action was possible. It demonstrated to some of the more timid local Negro leaders the possibilities of the future, while prompting those who had always favored greater activism to demand results immediately rather than in the foggy faraway *someday.*

The Mississippi Freedom Democratic Party was not officially a COFO project as such, but COFO conducted its mock elections and provided much of the planning for its activities. The Freedom Democrats' success at Atlantic City, which guarantees that the state Democratic Party must be open to Negro participation, was engineered in large measure by the work of COFO staff members and volunteers. They were handed their triumph by the apparent political death-wish of the official Mississippi delegation's spokesmen, who were singularly inept when it mattered most, but it was a triumph nonetheless.

COFO has not left Mississippi with the summer, although its ranks have been severely depleted by the return of most volunteers to college, pulpit or job. A state headquarters continues to operate in Jackson, and there are community projects all over the state. The National Council of Churches is fully embarked on its own attempt at social action, the Delta Ministry. This envisions a semi-permanent commitment to work in Mississippi in a far-ranging attack on all aspects of racial discrimination. COFO itself is sure that hundreds of volunteers can be expected again this summer, although the NAACP, one of COFO's ostensible constituent members, is publicly airing its displeasure at some of the organization's tactics.

No matter how many volunteers come to Mississippi again in the summer of 1965, it can be hopefully predicted that the intensity of the pattern of last summer will not be duplicated. Another book such as this will not be so easily produced again (and it should be added that the affidavits which were used were culled from a far larger number of similar incidents). Last summer's recurring violence plus the 1964 Civil Rights Act's imperatives, have at last freed some of the decent white men of Mississippi from their fearful acquiescence to brutality and from the necessity for silent dissent. People are at last speaking out against violence—individually and through their state and local organizations. The white majority still believes firmly in segregation, but some no longer in the preservation of segregation at any price. At least a few politicians are finding it expedient to echo the new moderate line for the first time, while that handful who have always done so are speaking more vigorously.

This attitude is an advance over the summer of 1964, when it was seemingly impossible for Mississippi's leaders to take a firm stand against murder, let alone against thoroughgoing defiance of the federal law and of human decency. There will be many Mississippians, thoroughly respectable men and women, who will try to forget that events such as those described in these pages ever occurred, or to pretend they did not. If it does nothing else, this book should provide an effective antidote to that hypocrisy and a vivid reminder to all Americans that the old truism is still valid: "All that is necessary for the triumph of evil is for good men to do nothing." It took a summer of shame for us in Mississippi to appreciate this warning. The elements of that shame are detailed in the affidavits which follow.

HODDING CARTER III

Mississippi Black Paper

United States Court of Appeals of Appeals for the Fifth Circuit

Council of Federated Organizations, et al.,

Petitioners—Appellants,

against

L.A. RAINEY, et al.,

HON. SIDNEY MIZE,

Respondent-Appellees

THE VERIFIED COMPLAINT IN THIS PLENARY SUIT WAS FILED ON JULY 10, 1964, with the Clerk of the United States District Court for the Southern District of Mississippi, Jackson Division, under Civil Action No. 3599 (J) (M), (Exhibit A). Service on defendants L. A. RAINEY (sued herein as L. C. RAINEY), CECIL PRICE, T. B. BIRDSONG and ASSOCIATION OF CITIZENS COUNCILS OF MISSISSIPPI (sued herein as WHITE CITIZENS COUNCILS OF MISSISSIPPI) has been effected.

The complaint prays for a permanent and temporary injunction against the use of "force, violence or any terroristic act" by the individual and organizational defendants and the five representative classes to deter the plaintiffs and the six classes they represent "from exercising their rights, privileges and immunities as citizens of the United States." In addition, it prays for an order directing the increase of United States Commissioners pursuant to the provisions of Title 42, U.S.C. §1989, so as to provide at least one to be stationed in the office of every sheriff in the 82 counties of the State of Mississippi, to arrest all persons violating "the laws of the United States protecting the civil rights of citizens and the elective franchise." . . .

The action below was brought because law and order have *completely and totally* broken down in Mississippi. The recent murders of the three civil rights workers only dramatized what this Court and almost everyone in the United States knows to be the tragic fact—namely, that life, person and property are in daily jeopardy throughout that state. In desperation, the Negroes of Mississippi and their white supporters have turned to the federal courts for the protection Congress has provided for such emergencies.

As the affidavits submitted in support of the motions for temporary injunctive relief below and for emergency relief in this Court clearly show, the defendants, or some of them, and their classes have, for years, brutalized the plaintiffs and their classes. Murders, bombings, burnings, beatings, terrorization and intimidation continue throughout the state at a steadily increasing tempo without any attempts by state or local authorities to prevent them. In many instances, the police themselves were—and are—directly involved or tacitly or openly encouraged—and encourage—the form of brutalization being employed.

The affidavits referred to above are presently before this Court. They may be summarized as follows:

A Approximately 90 affidavits as to illegal acts of Mississippi law enforcement officers against civil rights workers and the Negro citizens of Mississippi, including physical violence, intimidation, harassment, unprovoked arrests and prolonged unjustified incarceration which are daily continuing.

B Approximately 75 affidavits as to the murder, physical violence and other terroristic acts against civil rights workers and Negro citizens by white Mississippians which are daily continuing.

C Approximately 18 affidavits as to the burning or destruction by other means of churches and other buildings being used by civil rights workers and Negro citizens in connection with voter registration drives, protest meetings and other civil rights assemblies which are daily continuing.

D Approximately 35 affidavits as to the failure of Mississippi law enforcement officers to take any or adequate steps to safeguard civil rights workers and Negro citizens against physical violence and property destruction although fully warned in advance of the probability of their occurrence, all of which is daily continuing.

E Approximately 4 affidavits as to the misuse of power by members of the Mississippi judiciary in connection with the prosecution of civil rights workers and Negro citizens of Mississippi, all of which is daily occurring.

F Approximately 35 affidavits as to the failure of the law enforcement officers of Mississippi to prosecute known perpetrators of violence, destruction and terrorism against the persons and property of civil rights workers and Negro citizens, all of which is daily continuing....

Statements and Notarized Affidavits

COUNTY OF AMITE

I am 56 years old, a Negro, and a resident of Amite County, Mississippi. I have lived in Amite County all my life.

In 1954 I organized the Amite County Chapter of the NAACP. We held several meetings in Liberty, and in other places in Amite County. One night, while we were having a meeting in a school building in the 5th District of the county, the sheriff, Ira Jenkins, his deputy, and a member of the school board, and 15 or 20 other white men came out and surrounded the building. Then the sheriff, deputy, and school board member came into the meeting. This was about 8 P.M. These three did not take off their hats or anything, they just sat down. Then the school board member turned to different people and asked them what they were doing at the meeting. They didn't answer him. Then he said: "My advice to you is to take this money and put it into the school building." He apparently thought the group was collecting some money, though this was not the case. When they were ready to leave, the sheriff without asking reached on the table and took the secretary's book. Then they left the building and drove off. Because of their presence, the people were frightened and the meeting ended.

Ever since that time, whenever we have held meetings, the sheriff or his deputy drives around, and the people are frightened by this. We discuss voter registration at these meetings, and that is why they want to frighten us. It is hard to get people to come to the meetings because they are so afraid. Before 1954 it was easy to get people to any kind of meeting or to take part in any kind of organization.

I live very far off the highway, and the white people have never come out to threaten me at my house. But in September, 1963, a cross was burned where the road to my house leads off from the highway. I believe that the Ku Klux

Klan is operating in Amite County. It is extremely dangerous for anyone to work for civil rights there without protection from outside the county. We don't have any protection from inside the county—we can't depend on it there. I feel that my life is in danger. There is not an hour which passes when I do not feel my life is in danger. I have felt this since I began working for the NAACP in 1954, and it has gotten worse all the time. I feel this because I hear about people being beaten and threatened in Amite County. They do not say much, because they are afraid, and they do not have anyone they can appeal to for help.

SIGNED: *E. W. Steptoe*

HINDS COUNTY

I am a resident of Jackson, Negro, 22 years of age.

On July 5, 1961, I was in the Trailways bus station in Jackson, Mississippi, trying to get a ticket to New Orleans. Jackson police came up, asked me to move from the white section. I refused and the police hit me three times on the back of the neck with night sticks. This was during the Freedom Rides sponsored by CORE. I was then taken to city jail and charged with breach of the peace; and was eventually taken to the state penitentiary on conviction of $200 and four months. I served 45 days in the penitentiary. While I was still in city jail I had to see a doctor because my neck was bleeding from the beating in the Trailways station. The police allowed a doctor into the jail to give me treatment.

On March 9, 1962 (approximately), I went to the county courthouse in Jackson (Hinds County) to attend a trial of Diane Nash. I went into the courtroom and I took a seat on the so-called white side. I was approached by the bailiff of the court, asking me to move to the Negro side. I refused. The presiding judge, Russell Moore, then asked me to move from the bench. He stopped the trial for this purpose. I asked him why. He gave no reason and just said: "Are you going to move?" Then he said I was under arrest for contempt of court. I was then taken to county jail by the bailiff of the court. On the 22nd I had my trial. I had no lawyer. I asked Judge Russell Moore to continue my trial so that I could obtain a lawyer. He said: "Motion denied." I made another motion that he step down from the bench and have another judge in his place so he could take the witness stand and testify why he had placed me under arrest. He said: "Motion denied," again. He then put the bailiff on the witness stand, who testified that I had come into the court to start trouble and that I had been sitting "on the wrong side of the courtroom."

Then I asked the bailiff some questions. I asked him if he had authority to tell everyone in the courtroom where to sit and he said yes. Then I asked him why did he ask me to move. He said that the seats in my area had been reserved for some witnesses in the court. I then asked whether a white minister who had been sitting next to me and had come down from the North to observe the trial had been a witness. The bailiff said no. I asked why not. He said he had the right to ask whoever he wanted to move. Then he said: "We didn't want you to sit there." I then asked: "In other words the courtroom is segregated?" And he replied, "Yes." I then testified in my behalf. I said that my arrest had been unconstitutional, and that if released that day I would go right back into the courtroom and sit anywhere I pleased. I was then sentenced to $100 fine and 30 days on the county farm.

The bailiff who had testified was the one who took me back upstairs. And on our way back to the elevator, I asked him how long he had been working for the court.

He said: "None of your damn business." I then said: "You guys are pretty smart. First you segregate us, and then you testify against us in court and tell lies." At this point he got mad and called over three deputy sheriffs. He said: "Ride on up in the elevator with me. This nigger's trying to get tough." The deputies told me to put my hands up against the wall of the elevator. Then they started to beat me. They beat me with their fists until I fell to the floor. Then they began to kick me in the face and side. All four officers took part in the beating. When they put me in the cell, I was bleeding from my nose, above my eyes, and on the back of my neck. I asked for a doctor. The jailer refused to call one.

I was in the county jail for about a week and was then shifted to the county farm. I was singled out as a "troublemaker." I was the only prisoner there dressed in completely striped uniform, most prisoners being dressed in overalls and a T-shirt. I was told that if I was seen talking to anybody, the person that I talked to would be beaten. I was told that I must address all the guards as "Captain" and that if I didn't obey the guards' orders I would be punished.

I was assigned to the road gang, under a Captain _____. He asked me what I was in for. I said contempt of court. He said: "You're one of those god-damn Freedom Riders." I said I didn't know what that meant. He said: "Well, I'm going to have to whip your ass." Then he called four other prisoners and said: "Take this nigger to the woods, and we're going to whip his ass." They threw me on the ground and started pulling off my clothes. He took up a long hose pipe and hit me about fifteen times on the back, neck, buttocks, etc. Then he said, "Get up and put on your clothes." I asked him what he did that for. He said: "We always break in new people like that." Then I said: "I'm going to have to report you to the superintendent, and file a complaint with federal officials." Then he looked at the other prisoners and said: "Well, we got a smart nigger here." I laid back down and pulled off my clothes again and asked if he was going to beat me again. He said: "No, get up." When we got back to the county farm I asked to see the superintendent. He came in and asked me what I wanted. I told him what had happened. He asked me what I was going to do about it. I told him I wanted to file a complaint against the guard, and if he didn't do anything about it I would file a complaint against him. He asked me not to do that, and that if I did I would "catch hell." Then he left. He seemed both worried and mad. He pleaded with me not to file a complaint, but he shook and acted like he'd like to shoot me.

About a week later, the same guard asked me to move a three-hundred-pound log. I told him I wouldn't. He started to hit me with a big stick he picked up off the ground. He hit me fifteen or twenty times. I grabbed the stick out of his hand and threw it away and said that if he ever hit me again, "me and him was going to have it." He pulled out his gun and started backing up and shaking and saying: "Nigger, I ought to kill you." Then he put me in a truck and took me back to the county farm, and took me to the superintendent and told the superintendent that I had hit him. Then they put me in a car and brought me back to the county jail and threw me in solitary.

I was in solitary for 36 hours. The cell was 9 by 12, a "sweatbox." I was naked. The cell was a big steel vault in the ground, with no windows. They turned on heated air into the vault, and left it on all the time I was in the cell. Then they came back and took me back to the county farm. They started asking me questions, such as whether I was ready to "act right." I said, "If somebody treat me right." They said that everything would be okay.

Then they put me back on the same road gang. After about one week, the guard (Captain _____), pulled out a long hose pipe again and started to beat me one day without provocation. He struck me about 10 or fifteen times. I asked him why he had done that. He said: "You one of them smart-ass niggers. I don't like your ass." He took me back again to the county farm. I was put in a cell for about four days until I was released.

SIGNED: *Jesse Harris*

COAHOMA COUNTY

I am a Negro, 21 years old.

On February 6, 1962, when I was 19, I was walking with a young man down a Clarksdale street when Clarksdale police officers _____ and _____ stopped us and accused me of having been involved in a theft. I was taken to jail by the officers and they forced me to unclothe and lie on my back. One of the officers beat me between my legs with a belt. A few minutes later, the other officer began to beat me across my naked breasts.

SIGNED: *Bessie Turner*

COAHOMA COUNTY

I am a Negro and reside in Clarksdale, Mississippi. I genuinely support the motion aimed at bringing federal marshals into each county in Mississippi. This is because of many of my own experiences as president of the NAACP for the State of Mississippi and chairman of the Mississippi Council of Federated Organizations. I have had my life threatened by telephone, by carrier of word, and other means. A complaint has been filed with the NAACP, with the Civil Rights Commission, and with the Department of Justice, wherein a Mr. _____ signed an affidavit saying that a police officer of my home town had tried to get him to kill me.

On Good Friday of 1962, while sleeping in the dead of night, our home was bombed and set afire. In the house at that time besides my wife and daughter was Congressman Charles Diggs of the State of Michigan, now serving in the House of Representatives in Washington, D.C. The fact that he was staying with me had been circulated in the local paper, the Clarksdale *Press Register*, the day before. Immediately following that the house was fired upon with several slugs sticking in the walls. Three months after that, the Fourth Street Drug Store, my place of business, was bombed. The plate glass windows in the front of the store have been repeatedly broken out in the past few years. As a result of these many attacks, all of the insurance we have carried on the store and on our home has been canceled. Efforts are now being made to secure insurance.

On July 6, 1964, after spending the night in the Heidelberg Hotel in Jackson, on my way home my automobile became hot and stopped on the road. I had the car pulled into the Little Willie's Garage, which is my mechanic's. Upon examining the car, he found the motor frozen. Upon careful examination, he determined that sugar had been placed in my gas tank. It is my feeling that the sugar was placed in the tank while the car was overnight in the garage of the Heidelberg Hotel.

SIGNED: *Aaron Henry*

LEFLORE COUNTY

On Feb. 28, 1963, I attended a voter registration meeting in the office of the Student Nonviolent Coordinating Committee in Greenwood, Mississippi. At about 8:30 I noticed a white 1962 Buick circling the block. I checked further and discovered that there were no license plates on the car. At 10:15 that night, the car was still around the office and I notified the rest of the office people that it was still there and to be careful.

At about 10:30 that night, Robert Moses, Randolph Blackwell, and myself left the meeting to go to Greenville, Mississippi. The three of us first stopped at a gas station where we filled up the gas tank and got something to eat.

We then drove onto Highway 82 going to Greenville. As we were going onto the highway, we noticed the same white 1962 Buick that had been driving around the office coming off the highway. There were three white men in the car. As soon as they saw us, they turned around and pulled onto the highway behind us. I believe they were able to recognize us because our car had been parked in front of the SNCC office during the time they had been driving around it.

When I noticed their car following us on Highway 82, I slowed down to 35 m.p.h., the minimum speed limit on that 60 m.p.h. highway. I slowed down in order to let their car pass and also, if possible, to avoid being run off the road by them. When I slowed down, they also slowed down and remained behind us. They followed us for about seven miles, during all of which time there were many other cars on the road. At this point, there were no other cars in sight. They speeded up and pulled even with us. When they were right beside us, one of the men in the car opened fire with a submachine gun. He fired for about three or four seconds and then the car sped away.

I felt something hit me in the neck. I said, "I'm hit." Bob Moses, who was sitting beside me, grabbed the wheel from me and I then slumped in his lap.

Bob was able to stop the car safely. I was then taken and laid in the back seat. Randolph got into the back seat with me. Bob then drove to Itta Bena, which was the closest town. We knew that there was an infirmary at Mississippi Vocational College which was located there.

When we got there, there was no doctor present and we called to Greenwood to have one sent up. When he got there he took one look at me and told them to rush me to the hospital in Greenwood. I had been shot once in the neck and once in the shoulder. When our car was later examined, eleven to thirteen bullet holes were found in it.

I was then rushed to a Greenwood hospital where I stayed overnight, and then to Jackson, where the bullet that was still in me (a .45 caliber bullet) was removed from my neck. I stayed in the hospital two more days before I was released.

At the time I was shot, I was twenty years old and a field secretary for SNCC. Bob Moses was also a SNCC field secretary and Randolph Blackwell was the field director of the Voter Education Project being run by the Southern Regional Conference. All three of us are Negro.

SIGNED: *James Travis*

LEFLORE COUNTY

I am 24, Negro, and a resident of Cleveland, Mississippi.

On or about August 16, 1962, at about 12 P.M., I was at Burns' Studio at 616 Ave. I, in Greenwood. We had taken people to the courthouse that day to register to vote. We looked out the window and saw a police car with a radio on (Greenwood city police). They stayed in front of the building for about five minutes, then they drove away to the corner of Ave. I and Broad St., and five minutes after they had gone, another car drove up which I assumed was a 1962 Buick or Oldsmobile. One room of Burns' Studio served as the SNCC office at this time.

During the time that we saw the second car drive up, we could see the men in the car with guns, apparently shotguns, in their hands. We placed a call to John Doar of the Justice Department (I made the first call at about 12:15 A.M.). Lawrence Guyot and Luvaugn Brown were with me. I talked to Mr. John Doar and told him what was happening. He replied that he admitted that our lives were in danger, but the best thing he could tell us to do at the present time under these circumstances was for us to get out of the building and save our lives.

We took that advice because he said that the Justice Department could not really act until a federal statute had actually been violated. Luvaugn Brown saw the men getting out of the car and come around the side of the building up the back flight of stairs, which was the only way to enter the building at night (we were on the second floor).

We saw that the group, about 8 people in all, were very well armed with shotguns, ropes, bricks, chains, pistols, and other weapons. We knew that their intention was to kill us if they could find us in the building. We knew we had to get out of the building, so we crawled out of a bathroom window onto a neighboring roof. We crawled to the front of the building on our stomachs, and saw another car driving up (a '55 Chevrolet, probably blue), carrying other men who were armed the same way. We thought our best bet would be to get out of the community and the neighborhood to save our lives. The new earful of men also got out of their car. We went over another roof and down a TV antenna and were able to get away.

We went to the home of a Negro schoolteacher, employed by the Board of Education of Sunflower County. He said that he could not let us stay there because if he did he would probably lose his job. So he went to his father's house and asked his father to let us stay there. We stayed there and returned to the office about 6:30 or 7 A.M. and when we arrived found Bob Moses and Willy Peacock already there. The door had been kicked open, though it was locked, and records were all over the floor.

I had also called the FBI (Agent George E. Everett, in Greenwood since the Emmett Till case. He is now County District Attorney of Leflore County). I talked to him at about 12:15, right after calling John Doar. He said: "Well, Sam, you say the police were there. I'll go down to the police station and check and see if you are there [at the police station]. If you are not there, I'll perhaps come down to the office." He never came around that night to our knowledge, but he did come to the office between 8 and 10 A.M. the next morning.

At the time of this incident, I was a field secretary for SNCC.

SIGNED: _____*

*The publishers have been unable to locate the writer of this affidavit to secure his permission for its publication.

COAHAMA COUNTY

I am 16 years of age and was born in San Francisco, California. I presently reside in Clarksdale, together with my grandmother, Mrs. Beatrice Tanner. I have been a resident of Clarksdale for the last 15 years. My parents live in San Francisco. I also attend Clarksdale Agricultural High School.

On or about April 15, 1963, at approximately 7 P.M., I was walking alone, along Sunflower Avenue, Clarksdale, on my way home from Leon's Department Store, where I was working, when I was stopped by a Clarksdale police officer by the name of A_____. He told me to get into his car, which I did. He then started driving to city hall. En route he said that some "boy" had told him that I had stolen a car. This I denied. He then told me, "If you don't tell me the truth, I'll kill you." I then told him that in that event he would have to kill me. When we reached the jail, at Clarksdale City Hall, my shirt was torn off by one of five policemen, including B_____, C_____, and D_____. I was then told to get out of my clothes, which I did. While I was naked the same five police officers kicked, slapped, and punched me with their hands and feet. This beating lasted 35—40 minutes. I was hit in my face, buttocks, legs, and ear. Officer B_____ cuffed me on the left ear with the palm of his hand. When he pulled his hand away from my ear, it immediately began to ache. As a result of that beating and cuffing my left ear still periodically aches. It feels as if I can breathe through that ear, and water makes it ache. I never had that trouble before the aforementioned beating. I have not been to a doctor.

After the beating I was put into a cell. About 30 minutes later Officer B_____ came back and forced me to sign some papers called an "affidavit," which I didn't read. I spent the rest of the night in jail. The next week I was taken to city court. I had been in jail up until then with no visitors and no lawyer. At the court, I pleaded guilty to possessing a stolen car, a 1955 Chevrolet. Three other boys, Sonny, Roosevelt, and June were also convicted. (I was and still am innocent of the charge. I had been in said car only once, and that was about two days before the aforementioned arrest, and that was when Sonny drove the aforementioned car over to my house and said: "Look what my mother bought me." I then rode in the car with Sonny for about an hour and a half. I did not know that it was stolen. After riding, Sonny dropped me off at Henry Lawrence's grocery store, Poplar and Jefferson Aves., then he drove off with the car.) I was sentenced to one year imprisonment and $500 fine and served eight months.

About one week after I began serving my sentence I was whipped, beaten, and assaulted a second time. This was done by Police Officer E_____. He used a long leather strap about three feet in length and whipped me on the buttocks. This beating lasted about 15 minutes. The next beating came about a month later and was administered by Police Officer E_____ and Police Officer F_____ with the aforementioned leather strap on my buttocks with no clothes. This beating lasted about 10 minutes and resulted from my refusal to inform on another prisoner. The next beating occurred about two weeks later. This time Officer G_____ punched me with his fists in and about the face, head, and mouth. He broke my left upper front tooth. This beating resulted from my having asked Officer G_____ to leave a particular door open. The last beating occurred about two months later, about 8:30 P.M. Officer E_____ again whipped me with a leather strap on my neck and buttocks for about 15 minutes. He had accused me of "rambling" through the mayor's office.

In September, 1963, I reported the above incidents to the Clarksdale FBI in person.

SIGNED: *Larry Johnson*

LEFLORE COUNTY

I am 24, Negro, and a resident of Cleveland, Mississippi.

On or about March 6, 1963, I, Willie Peacock, Mrs. Essie Broom, and Peggy Marye had been sorting food and clothing that had been sent from Chicago at the Wesley Chapel Methodist Church on the corner of Howard and Gibbs St. in Greenwood, Mississippi. The food and clothing had been sent down because the Board of Supervisors of Leflore County had held an open meeting and invited all white citizens in Leflore County to attend. The meeting was held sometime before March 6 and at the meeting distribution of surplus commodities was the topic. One man made the motion that distribution of surplus foods be discontinued. His name was Mr. _____, president of a local bank. It was voted on and was approved 49–21. So food distribution was stopped.

We started our own food drive to aid local Negroes who had been intimidated and harassed for attempting to register to vote. Approximately 22,000 people were cut off from surplus food by the decision to end distribution. This statistic comes from the statistics of the welfare rolls of Leflore County. Less than 1% of those cut off from surplus food distribution were white.

On March 6, 1963, we had been sorting the first large shipment of food and clothing we had received since beginning a drive in the North to obtain commodities by donation.

After sorting the food and clothing, about 11 P.M. we drove back to the SNCC office at 115 E. McLaurin St., in Greenwood. I did not see a car behind us, though I constantly looked out the rear view mirror in the car, which I was driving. We had told others earlier in the evening that our car might be shot into because the men who had shot into Jimmy Travis' car on February 28, 1963, had been released from jail that day (March 6, 1963).

About two seconds after arriving in front of the SNCC office, a car drove up and fired into our car before we could get out. We were shot at with deer slugs from a double-barreled shotgun. The shots knocked the windows out of both front doors of the car. There were only two shots. After getting out of the car, I saw the car drive off very slowly. It was a station wagon without license plates.

Willie Peacock called the police, and they arrived fifteen minutes later. They talked to Mrs. Essie Broom. The police said: "Don't you know that you didn't have any business being in the car with that nigger?" He said: "That nigger is the most dangerous nigger in Mississippi." He said: "If you don't watch out, that nigger's going to get you killed. You'd better stop riding with him." She said: "Yes, sir." The police looked around the car.

They said we had plotted the shooting to receive cheap publicity. Some of them proceeded to leave.

The police took us to the hospital, where we were treated for slight injuries from glass fragments and for shock. We were then taken to the city hall and were questioned there by the FBI.

Then we were taken back to the office and the FBI came out the next morning and found between ten and seventeen slugs in the side of a lady's house across from the office, where we had been parked.

SIGNED: _____*

*The publishers have been unable to locate the writer of this affidavit to secure his permission for its publication.

COAHOMA COUNTY

I am a Negro, 38 years old, and I reside with my husband in Clarksdale, Mississippi.

I am secretary of the Coahoma County NAACP, and on April 23, 1963, I was beaten by Mr. _____, _____ Service Station attendant, because I asked to use the service station rest room while they were servicing my car. He also refused to return my change, and because I refused to stop asking for my change back, this was an additional reason he began to beat me.

After I returned home, I called the office of Police Officer A_____ and reported the incident, and asked that Officer A_____ get in touch with me. About 50 minutes later, he came to my house with a warrant for my arrest for "disturbing the peace," and arrested me. I had to post a bond in order to seek medical treatment.

On June 8, 1963, about twenty minutes to one in the morning, while I was in bed, someone shot into our house, and the bullet was recovered from under the piano. Officer B_____ investigated the incident but no one has been arrested.

SIGNED: *Vera Mae Pigee*

HINDS COUNTY

I was arrested on June 1, 1963, at approximately 3:45 in the afternoon by two unidentified members of the Jackson Police Department.

At the time of my arrest I was standing on the lawn of a Negro residence on Pascagoula Street watching an anti-segregation demonstration. I saw a policeman hit a demonstrator whom I identified as David Green, who resides on _____ Street in Jackson. I pointed to the beating and a cop yelled out, "Get him!" Three policemen came onto the lawn and grabbed me and took me down into the street. A few seconds after I had been hustled onto the street a policeman hit me in my back with a billy stick. We stood in the street for approximately ten minutes. I was not informed as to why I was being held in custody. The officers did not tell me I was under arrest until after I was searched in the street.

En route to the police car I was being escorted by Officers A_____ and B_____. One of these officers kept stepping on my heels. I asked him to stop. The other officer slammed the door on my ankle as I was getting into the police car. We sat in the police car for a period of five to ten minutes. We then started toward the city jail. A policeman whom I believe to have been Officer A_____ called the police headquarters via short wave radio and asked what to do with me. The officer was told, "If you can't connect him with the demonstrations, turn him loose." The calling officer replied, "Officer C_____ told me to arrest him." The person on the other end of the intercom system said, "Take him to the 'kalaboo.'" The officer seated beside me then started to beat me with his billy stick. We were at this point passing the city jail.

I was then taken to an alley approximately one block from the State Capitol. The officers stopped the car. The officer seated beside me then started to beat me on the head with a billy club. The officer who was driving the car got out of the car and came around and opened the door on the side where I was sitting and pulled me out of the car onto the ground. All the while this was occurring the officer seated beside me was continually beating me on the head. The officer who pulled me out of the car stomped me in the stomach three times while I was lying on the ground. As I attempted to raise myself up I was stomped on the hands by Officer A_____. Officer A_____ then said, "Nigger, get back in the car." I got back in the car with my head bleeding badly. Officer A_____ said, "That's nigger blood." I told the officers that one of the reasons why we were demonstrating was because of police brutality. The officer who was driving the car said, "You damn niggers are demanding too much and you ain't going to get it!" We then pulled off. Upon stopping at an intersection, another police car full of officers said, "What happened to him? Did he fall?" The officer riding on the front seat said, "Yes, he fell."

We went down Jefferson St. and turned left, ending up one block from High Street heading toward the city hall. The officer seated beside me hit me between the eyes with a billy stick. We then proceeded to the city jail. The officer in the back seat told me to get out of the car. I got out of the car. The officer on the back seat started beating me on my leg which had began to swell and automatically lifted off the ground.

I was then taken to the police booking room where I complained to Officer C_____ about my having been beaten. Officer C_____ started making excuses for the officers and accused me of resisting arrest. The policemen except one and the jailer (Mr. _____) went into another room and came out and told me that I was charged with "resisting arrest" and two other charges which they did not quote to me. I was then taken to a cell after I was permitted to make one phone call.

The following day, June 2, 1963, one attorney from the United States Department of Justice visited me and I gave him the story of what had happened. The FBI came down later the same day and took some pictures and an affidavit.

I was released on June 3, 1963, at 7 P.M. No date for my trial has been set, nor do I know what the other two charges against me are. I was released on a $200 appearance bond.

I hereby authorize the U.S. Department of Justice and the NAACP to proceed in any way under the Constitution to protect and guarantee the rights of black Americans in Mississippi from further beatings of this kind.

SIGNED: *James Wilson Jones*

COAHOMA COUNTY

I am a Negro, 41 years old. I reside in Clarksdale, Coahoma County, Mississippi.

I am a member of the Clarksdale NAACP and as a part of our program of awakening the conscience of the church community to support the need for establishing a bi-racial community, I led a group of five pickets at the largest white church in Clarksdale on June 9th, 1963, Father's Day.

At the time above, I was employed at _____'s Cafe, on _____ Ave., in Clarksdale, Mississippi, by Mrs. _____. Later, when she heard about it, she said that she didn't blame me, since I was doing this for the betterment of my race, and that she would have done the same.

The next week, two police officers came to the cafe. One of them was Officer A _____. He delivered a message from Officer B_____ that I had to be rid of in an hour or he will have the city health department close the cafe. I saw the officers come and saw them talk to Mrs. _____, and after they left, she told me what they said above. She then gave me my money and I left.

It is my serious belief that the only reason I and Mrs. _____ had to terminate my job is because Officer B _____ arrested my group which had been picketing the church on Father's Day, and charged me with "parading without a permit," and I had to give where I worked when I was booked.

For 6 months I looked for a job. Always before I had worked steady, working for particular employers 3 to 4 years at a time. After I had been "fired" by Mrs. _____ I would get a job, but after a day or two, my new employer would come to me and say, "You are a member of the NAACP!" and make me quit.

SIGNED: *Hattie Mae Gilmore*

MONTGOMERY COUNTY

I am a Negro, 46 years of age, and reside in Ruleville, Sunflower County.

On the 9th of June, 1963, I, Miss Annell Ponder, and eight other women were returning from a voter registration workshop in South Carolina. We were on a Continental Trailways bus that stopped at Winona, Montgomery County, at the bus station. Annell Ponder and others of our party, including James West from Itta Bena, Rosemary Freeman from near Greenwood, and June Johnson, a 15-year-old girl, got off the bus to go to the restaurant. Two, Euvester Simpson and Ruth Day, also of our party, got off the bus to use the rest room. I remained on the bus.

The four that got off the bus to go to the restaurant—and had gone to the "white" side of the restaurant—were coming back to the bus. I got off the bus and asked them what happened. They said that there were some policemen and highway patrolmen in there. Annell said policemen with billy clubs told them to get out of there. I said that this can be reported and Annell said, "Yes, I am going to get the tag number." The four of them were standing outside to get the tag number, and Euvester Simpson was standing with them talking, when all five of them were put in the patrol car, which I think was the highway patrolman's car; he was also the one giving orders.

I got off the bus when all at once an officer from the patrol car said, "Get that one too." A county deputy, Officer A_____, and one more got out of the car and opened the door to his car and said, "You are under arrest." I was going into the car when Officer A_____ kicked me into the car. While driving me to the jail, they were questioning me and calling me "bitch."

We got to the jail, and I saw all five of the above [Annell Ponder, Rosemary Freeman, June Johnson, James West, and Euvester Simpson] in the booking room. As soon as I got to the booking room, a tall policeman walked over to James West and jumped hard on James West's feet.

I was led into a room—a cell—with Euvester Simpson. While I was in the cell, I could hear screaming and the passing of kicks. Pretty soon I saw several white men bringing Annell Ponder past my cell. She was holding on to the jail walls, her clothes all torn, her mouth all swelled up, and her eyes were all bloody—only one eye looking like itself.

After a while they came for me: Officer B_____, a highway patrolman (his name on a metal plate on his pocket); the policeman who had jumped on James West's feet; and another policeman with a crew-cut haircut.

They came into my cell and asked me why I was demonstrating, and said that they were not going to have such carryings-on in Mississippi. They asked me if I had seen Martin Luther King, Jr. I said I could not be demonstrating—I had just got off the bus—and denied that I had seen Martin Luther King. They said "Shut up" and always cut me off. They then asked me where I was from. I said Ruleville. They then left, saying that they were going to check it out.

They then returned. Officer B_____ said: "You damn right you are from Ruleville. We are going to make you wish that you were dead, bitch." They led me to another cell. Before I had been led out of the cell, I saw a Negro—who I reckoned was a trusty, who stayed around the jail—bring a mop and bucket to take somewhere. Doctor Searcy, Cleveland, Mississippi, said that I had been beaten so deeply that my nerve endings are permanently damaged, and I am sore.

SIGNED: *Fannie Lou Hamer*

MONTGOMERY COUNTY

I am 31, Negro, and a resident of Atlanta, Georgia.

I was returning on June 9, 1963, from a workshop in voter education and community development held in John's Island, South Carolina. I was returning on a Trailways bus together with Mrs. Fannie Lou Hamer, June Johnson, Euvester Simpson, James West, Rosemary Freeman, and four other people.

When we got to the Winona bus station at about 12 noon, the five people named above, excepting Mrs. Hamer, got off the bus, and June Johnson, James West, and Rosemary Freeman and I went into the lunchroom. This lunchroom was the one normally reserved for white people (all of the party were Negroes). We sat down at the counter and the waitress behind the counter wadded up some paper and threw it against the wall and said: "I can't take no more."

By this time a member of the Winona city police (apparently _____) and a member of the highway patrol entered the back of the room. They came up behind where we were sitting and tapped each of us on the shoulders and said: "Get up and get out of here." I was the last one on the line, and I asked him if he didn't know it was against the law to put us out. (This was after the ICC ruling against discrimination in ICC facilities.) He said: "Ain't no damn law, get up and get out of here."

So we went outside. We stood outside discussing what happened. Mrs. Hamer saw us and got off the bus and asked us why we had come out so quick. So we told her what happened, and she said: "Yeah, this is what we have to put up with. This is what we have to go against here in Mississippi."

Then we agreed that we would include what had happened here in a report we were going to make about incidents during the trip. Mrs. Hamer got back on the bus and the rest of us stayed in front of the station talking, saying that it didn't look good to get up and walk out of the lunchroom when we knew we had a right to be in there. We said if anything like that happened again, we would just go to jail.

Then I went back to the door and looked inside to get a better look at the police officers, so I could identify them. But they crouched back against the wall so I couldn't see them. So I decided I would get the number off the patrolman's car. It didn't have a number on the side so we walked around to the back, to get the license plate number.

As I was taking that down, the officers came out of the restaurant and said that we were under arrest, and said: "You all get in that car," indicating the highway patrol car. Mrs. Hamer saw us getting in the car and she got off the bus, and she called out to me and asked me what I wanted them to do. I told her to go ahead on the bus.

The officer driving the car we were in called out to another policeman and said: "Get that other one too." Mrs. Hamer was then placed in another car which followed us to the Montgomery County Jail.

When we got there they started questioning us and one of them asked me something and I said "Yes" or "No." Then he wanted to know if I had enough "respect" for him to say "sir" when I answered his questions. So I asked him what he said, and he repeated his question, using the term "nigger" to refer to me. I told him I didn't know him that well. He looked very angry and confused. Then the highway patrol man walked over and stepped hard on James West's foot and ground on it, though James had not done anything.

Then they questioned us more about the civil rights work, about the Greenwood voter registration project, and said we had come to demonstrate. After a while they put us in cells, two of us together in a cell. James West and June Johnson were kept out.

After we were in awhile, I heard them questioning June Johnson, asking her what did she think they were supposed to do about it, apparently referring to our presence in Winona and our activities in civil rights. June said that she felt they were supposed to protect us and take care of us. Then I began to hear sounds of violence. There was a whiskey still (metal) in the booking room and I could hear people scraping against this and the floor and walls, and could hear June screaming.

After a while they came to get me, bringing June to put in my cell. She was bleeding from the face and neck and crying. They took me into the booking room, and made me stand several different places consecutively. Finally I was standing in a corner. There was blood on the floor in this place. I started to tell the four white men and police officers in the room that we wanted them to understand that we didn't hate them. When I told them that they turned toward me and one of them (in blue uniform) said he wanted to hear me say "sir." I ignored him. Another young man in a crew-cut said: "You just came up here to stir up trouble." The man slapped me in the head with his fist. Then the officer in blue uniform hit me. Then the highway patrolman wanted to know why I took down his license plate number. I told him I wanted to make an accurate report if there was trouble. They wanted to know who we would make a report to. I told him the federal government.

They said: "Who do you mean, Bobby Kennedy?" and there was contempt in their voices. I said: "No, the federal government." Then they started again insisting I say "sir." Through all this conversation they kept hitting me. The policeman in blue uniform at one point took a sort of blackjack from the man who I believe was _____ and from then on he used that in beating me. This went on for about 10 minutes, with questioning and my being beaten to the floor and getting up and being beaten down again. At one point the highway patrolman hit me in the stomach. They finally stopped beating me and put me in a maximum security cell. One of my teeth had been chipped and my lip was bleeding, and later when I tried to walk I staggered and fell.

When I was brought to another cell I saw two Negroes who were in their 20s or a little younger. Officer B_____ said, "Take this," talking to the youngest Negro. Officer B_____ had in his hand a long, 2-foot blackjack made out of leather, wider at one end, and one end being filled with something heavy. The young Negro said: "You mean for me to beat her with this?" Officer B_____ said, "You damn right. If you don't, you know what I will do for you."

The young Negro told me to get on the bunk and he began to beat me. I tried to put my hands to my side where I had polio when I was a child, so that I would not be beat so much on that side. The first Negro beat me until he got tired. Then the second Negro was made to beat me. I took the first part of it, but couldn't stand the second beating. I began to move and the first Negro was made to sit on my feet to keep me from kicking. I remember that I tried to smooth my dress which was working up from all of the beating. One of the white officers pushed my dress up. I was screaming and going on, and the young officer with the crew-cut began to beat me about the head and told me to stop my screaming. I then began to bury my head in the mattress and hugged it to kill out the sound of my screams. It was impossible to stop the screaming. I must have passed out—I remember trying to raise my head and heard one of the officers, Officer B_____, who said, "That's enough."

He said, "Get up and walk." I could barely walk. My body was real hard, feeling like metal. My hands were navy blue, and I couldn't bend the fingers. I was taken back to the cell.

While I was back in the cell, I could talk to June Johnson, Annell Ponder, and Rosemary Freeman, who were in their cells. I learned that June Johnson had a hole in her head from her beating. I learned that the trusty had used the bucket and mop to mop the blood.

Then they got us up one night to take our pictures and Officer B_____, who had taken the pictures, forced me to sign a statement which they already had made me write, that I had been treated all right. That night was the following Monday night. I tried to write the statement in such a way that anybody would know that I had been forced to write the statement.

The following Tuesday, we had our trial. There was no jury. We had no lawyer.

We were charged and were found guilty of disorderly conduct and resisting arrest.

When we were put in the jail, and when I was put in the jail, I told them that nothing is right around here. The arresting officer had lied and said that I was resisting arrest. I told them that I was not leaving my cell, and that if they wanted me they had to kill me in the cell and drag me out. I would rather be killed inside my cell instead of outside the cell.

On that Tuesday, I heard some white men talk to Officers C_____ and D_____ and that they were FBI and had to report what they said. I was able to see Lawrence Guyot, a field secretary of SNCC who I had known before in voter registration work, and saw him in the booking room and saw that he had been beaten.

On the following Wednesday, James Bevel, Andrew Young, and Dorothy Cotton of SCLC (Southern Christian Leadership Conference) came to see us and to get us (the people who had been on the bus and were arrested) out. But before I left the jail I was able to see that Lawrence Guyot's head had been beaten out of shape.

On the 31st of August, 1962, I had been fired from my plantation job, Dee Marlow's Plantation, Ruleville, because I attempted to register to vote. I had been working for SNCC and SCLC before I had been beaten. At the present time, I am a candidate for Congress in the coming primary, for the Second Congressional District.

I was kept in the cell for three days and no doctor was brought to see me.

After three days I was charged in a trial with disorderly conduct and resisting arrest. We were found guilty, and appealed. And the next day we were released. We would have been fined $100 on each charge, but we got out on $200 appeal bond.

Since then the Justice Department brought suit against the officers. They denied the charge and an all-white male jury found them innocent.

SIGNED: *Annell Ponder*

MONTGOMERY COUNTY

I am 16 years old and live in Greenwood, Mississippi. A group of civil rights workers was traveling from Charleston, South Carolina, to Greenwood, Miss., by bus on June 9, 1963. The group consisted of Mrs. Fannie Lou Hamer, Miss Annell Ponder, Mr. James West, Miss Euvester Simpson, Miss Rosemary Freeman, and myself. On the trip from Columbus, Miss., to Winona, Miss., our group sat in the front of the bus and occasionally sang freedom songs.

When we got to Winona, the bus stopped at the terminal there. Everybody went into the terminal except Mrs. Hamer. When we got inside the terminal, our group sat down on the "white" side. [A] Winona [police officer] came in and told us to "get over where you belong." We got up and went outside the terminal. Soon the [police officer] and a state trooper came outside and arrested us. When she saw us getting into the trooper's car, Mrs. Hamer got out of the bus and asked us, "Should I go on to Greenwood?" We told her to go ahead, but the trooper called out, "Get that woman," and an unidentified white man grabbed her and put her in his car. The trooper took us to the Montgomery County Jail. Mrs. Hamer arrived in the other car about the same time.

We were taken inside. The trooper said, "What you niggers come down here for—a damn demonstration?" We all shook our heads and answered "No." Then he said, "You damn niggers don't say 'No' to me—you say 'Yes, sir.'" While he was saying this, Officer A_____ and the Winona [police officer] came in, accompanied by the same white man that brought Mrs. Hamer in.

Officer A_____ walked over and stamped James West's toe and hit Euvester in the side with a ring of heavy keys. Then the trooper questioned us. While questioning Annell Ponder, he found out that she lived in Atlanta, Ga. He told her, "I knew you wasn't from Mississippi 'cause you don't know how to say 'Yes, sir' to a white man." Then he turned to the rest of us and said, "I been hearing about you black sons-of-bitches over in Greenwood, raising all that hell. You come over here to Winona, you'll get the hell whipped out of you."

He opened the door to the cell block and told everybody to get inside. I started to go in with the rest of them and he said, "Not you, you black-assed nigger." He asked me, "Are you a member of the NAACP?" I said yes. Then he hit me on the cheek and chin. I raised my arm to protect my face and he hit me in the stomach. He asked, "Who runs that thing?" I answered, "The people." He asked, "Who pays you?" I said, "Nobody." He said "Nigger, you're lying. You done enough already to get your neck broken." Then the four of them—Officer A_____, the [Winona police officer], the state trooper, and the white man that had brought Mrs. Hamer in—threw me on the floor and beat me. After they finished stomping me, they said, "Get up, nigger." I raised my head and the white man hit me on the back of the head with a club wrapped in black leather. Then they made me get up. My dress was torn off and my slip was coming off. Blood was streaming down the back of my head and my dress was all bloody. They put me in a cell with Rosemary Freeman, and called Annell Ponder. I couldn't see what they did to Annell, but I could hear them trying to make her say "Yes, sir." When they brought her back, she was bloody and her clothes were torn.

About 5 minutes later the trooper came in and yanked Rosemary Freeman off the bed and bumped her up against the brick wall of the cell two or three times. Then he turned to me and said, "Pull your dress down and wash off. When I come back in 5 minutes, you'd better be clean." I started to wash up but a man in a blue uniform told me to wait until we left.

Then we heard the policemen shouting at Mrs. Hamer in her cell. Then they took her somewhere into a different part of the building.

A little while later we heard Mrs. Hamer hollering, "Don't beat me no more, don't beat me no more." Later they brought her back to her cell crying. She cried at intervals during the night, saying that the leg afflicted with polio was hurting her terribly.

We stayed in that jail day and night from Sunday till Tuesday, when they booked us and informed us that we were charged with disorderly conduct and resisting arrest. We then went back to jail until Wednesday afternoon, when a group of SNCC people came from Greenwood to get us out of jail. We got back to Greenwood about 7 P.M. on June 12, 1963.

SIGNED: *June E. Johnson*

LEFLORE COUNTY

I am a native of Kosciusko, Mississippi, and am engaged in voter registration activity for the Student Nonviolent Coordinating Committee and the Council of Federated Organizations.

On June 25, 1963, I and fellow workers brought 200 people to the courthouse in Greenwood, Mississippi, Leflore County, to attempt to register to vote. A city ordinance was passed that same day that the people at the courthouse had to go home between 11:30 A.M. and 1 P.M. Some people had come from 30 miles away. At 11:30 we were told to move off the courthouse grounds. We moved down onto the sidewalk, and then were told by city police to disperse.

We then went back to the courthouse. The sheriff then came and arrested nine people whom he thought were the leaders. I was among those arrested. At 12 noon we were taken to jail.

At 1:30 P.M. that same day we were given a five-minute trial during which we were not given the opportunity to obtain an attorney. We were all convicted of disturbing the peace, and were sentenced to four months at hard labor on the county farm, and $200 fine. During the trial, the sheriff refused to answer relevant questions I asked.

While in the Leflore County Farm, we were always taken out to a place away from other prisoners, and groups of policemen and civilians would come and harass us verbally.

One day a guard pulled a pistol and cocked and pointed it at me when I asked him respectfully to call me by my name. All of us stopped moving, because it was obvious he would shoot somebody if they moved. We went on a work and hunger strike at noon that day, saying that we couldn't work under those conditions. As a result, we were all sent to Parchman State Penitentiary three days later.

On approximately July 15, while at Parchman, 14 prisoners, including myself, were told we were making too much noise, which we weren't, and were put in the "hot box," which is a room six feet square with no windows and no light and only a ventilation hole with a fan which was not running. Our only air came from a crack under the door. We were kept there for 40 hours. During that time Jimmy Pruitt became sick and collapsed with a fever. We requested help and after two hours the guards removed him. By that time, four others were sick and requested water. After three hours, we were given water. At that time, the fan was turned on. Pruitt was given a pill but no medical examination, although he had a high fever.

On approximately July 20, Willie Carnell was hung by his hands to the cell bars for 30 hours. Guards accused him of "singing."

On August 18 at 2 P.M., I was "sentenced" to hang similarly for 48 hours. I had done nothing. I actually hung for 3 hours.

When we were finally bailed out, Sergeant A_____ at Parchman told us that if any of us came back, he would shoot him. We had been in Parchman 55 days.

On November 3, in McComb, Mississippi, I was canvassing for the mock election. Police followed me wherever I went, stood beside me on the front porches of people, photographing them and taking their names while I was talking to them. I was continually detained and threatened by police for nothing. Police Chief Guy was in charge at that time.

During the last part of February of 1964, George Green and I were doing voter registration work in Natchez, Mississippi. We were arrested while stopped in our car, waiting for a train to pass. The charge was "investigation of auto theft" but after being detained 30 hours, I was charged with vagrancy and Green with speeding. During a week and a half we were picked up 5 times, usually without being arrested or questioned, and detained for 2 or more hours.

SIGNED: *Douglas MacArthur Cotton*

COAHOMA COUNTY

On July 30, 1963, at approximately 3 P.M., I was in the presence of nine other adult Negro citizens arrested by an unidentified police officer, and a few minutes later rearrested by Clarksdale Police Officer A_____. At the time of our arrest we were wearing anti-segregation signs and orderly moving down Sharkely Avenue toward the Clarksdale City Hall. The unidentified police officer who first placed us under arrest did not ask us if we had a permit to parade nor did he inform us as to what we were being charged with. In our second encounter, with Police Officer A_____, we were asked if we had a permit to parade. We told the officer we did not have a permit and that the request for a permit had been denied.

We were taken to the Clarksdale City Jail and charged with "parading without a permit."

Between 20–25 female demonstrators were placed in a 9 by 9 cell which I feel would normally house six or eight persons. We were not given any food on this date of our arrest. The following day, July 31, 1963, we were served for breakfast one spoonful of cold grits with no salt and one slice of cold bread. A group of young female demonstrators were taken out of the cell, leaving approximately eight of us in the cell.

Prior to the removing of the young demonstrators from the cell we had suffered severe discomfort due to the overcrowded conditions and excessive heat. On the night of July 31st, the conditions became worse as the heat was turned on. My hair was as if it had been washed, and sweat rolled down my face like rain.

Different police officers would come by at different times and call us ugly names like "nigger," "bitch," "cow," etc. Police officers were always violating our privacy by peeping in the cell saying, "Man, if we could get in there. Nigger women have some good _____."

On August 1, 1963, we were tried and convicted of "parading without a permit" and sentenced to thirty days in jail plus a $101 fine. Even though I was not in the court at the time of the trial I understand that a plea of *nolo contendere* was entered for me by my attorney, R. Jess Brown, of Jackson, Mississippi. I had understood this plea to be the legal position of our group prior to my participation in the peaceful protest.

On the evening of August 1, 1963, I requested a couple of aspirins because I was feeling very ill because of the excessive heat and poor food. I was told by a police officer, "If niggers were not so hot-headed they would not be in here." I was finally given the aspirins.

On August 2, 1963, at approximately 10 in the morning, Officer A_____ came to our cell and asked us if we thought this was a hotel, that we had to work. We were made to work in the heat of the day cutting grass with sling blades and hoes in the oil-mill area of town. We were ordered to work under the threat that if we did not work we would be taken back to the cell and the heat would be turned on again.

I became very ill because of the excessive heat and the poor food. I was taken back to the city jail and treated by the jail doctor despite the fact that I had asked to be treated by my own doctor. I understood there were rumors that I had suffered a heat stroke.

On August 3, 1963, at approximately 5:30 in the evening I was released from the city jail by posting a $400 bond. I was immediately taken to the Sarah Brown Memorial Hospital at Mound Bayou, Mississippi, where I remained for one week.

I am asking the NAACP and its legal staff to represent me in filing whatever legal action that may be necessary to punish those who have violated my rights while I was a prisoner in the Clarksdale City Jail. I am also requesting that the U.S. Department of Justice take the actions necessary to secure and protect my rights as an American citizen.

SIGNED: *Odessa Brooks*

COAHOMA COUNTY

I am twenty years old and a field secretary for the Student Nonviolent Coordinating Committee. I have been working in Clarksdale, Mississippi, for approximately two and one half months.

On August 9, 1963, between the hours of 10 o'clock and 1 o'clock P.M., I was arrested in the city of Clarksdale by two unidentified police officers and charged with violating the city's anti-littering ordinance. At the time of my arrest I had in my possession some leaflets announcing a mass meeting to be held on August 9, 1963. Along with me was Harold Supriano and Terrance Hallinan, both of whom are employed by the Student Nonviolent Coordinating Committee. We were working on Adams Street in a Negro area of town. At the time of my arrest I was not passing out any of the leaflets in my possession.

After my arrest I was charged with violating the city's anti-littering ordinance and taken to the Clarksdale City Jail. While I was being booked an officer asked me if I had been in the army. I told the officer I had not been in the army; at the moment of my reply the officer who was booking me stood up and struck me with great force in the stomach, and then stated, "If you had been in the army you would be able to take that."

Moments later six officers, including Police Officer A_____, came in and said, "I like to beat niggers' asses." The group of officers then surrounded me and began to beat me in the stomach and elsewhere. I took this beating for a brief time; then I blacked out. One of those persons with me said they beat me for approximately ten minutes. I was then taken to a cell in the city jail. Approximately two hours later two Coahoma County officers took me from my city jail cell and took me to the county jail after I had been handcuffed.

I remained in the county jail for approximately two hours, then I was taken back to the city jail, where I was released for the sum of $201.

I hereby authorize the NAACP and the U.S. Department of Justice to pursue and utilize any legal actions they may deem necessary to prevent the reoccurrence of such incidents to other citizens.

SIGNED: *Lafayette Surney*

PIKE COUNTY

I am a Negro participant in civil rights and desegregation work.

On January 15th, 1964, about 8 P.M., my children, Anne Marie, Melvin, Marilyn, Edward, and Earle, were watching television when they heard shots and saw particles of glass from our living room picture window fall to the floor. The children called my wife and told her what had happened. I came in shortly afterwards and called the police and talked with the constable, who said that "there wouldn't be no need of my coming tonight, because there wouldn't be nothing I could do," and that "I'll see you when I get back from Jackson." This happened on Wednesday. The next evening my shoe shop was shot into and my windows were broken. My sons were in the shop working at the time of the shooting, which was around 5 P.M. The constable and the sheriff came to see me at the shop Friday, the 17th of January. The sheriff told me that they had caught the boys and taken their guns. Later that evening the local police came and asked me whether I wanted to press charges or get paid for the damage. He said [a police officer] had told him to ask me which one, and I said that I want to get paid for the damage, because I knew if I had brought charges against them, I would not have gotten anything for the damage to my house and shop. I gave them an estimate of the damage, which was about $35, and I received this not long afterwards.

SIGNED: _____*

*The publishers have been unable to locate the writer of this affidavit to secure his permission for its publication.

COAHOMA COUNTY

On August 29, 1963, around 11 A.M., I was walking north on Fourth Street opposite Brocatos' Curb Market in Clarksdale, Mississippi, with another boy named R. T. Smith. I had returned the day before from the March on Washington, and still had on a T-shirt that was worn during the march. The shirt had the words "Freedom Now" across the back.

While walking north on Fourth Street at this point I was arrested by two members of the Clarksdale Police Department. The arresting officers were Officers A_____ and B_____.

I was charged with parading without a permit because of the wording on the back of my shirt. I was carried to the Clarksdale City Jail. After I was carried to the city jail I was booked by Officer A_____. While he was booking me he began to kick me between my legs and he slapped me several times. I did not attempt to fight back. I took his blows and said nothing. Officer A_____ gave Officer B_____ a blackjack and told me if I looked hard, for Officer B_____ to beat hell out of me across my head. He then carried me to the cell. He tried to slam the cell door on me but I moved fast and the door missed me.

I was booked for parading without a permit, vagrancy (being without a job), and resisting arrest. The resisting arrest charge grew out of my answering Officer A_____ "No," when he insisted upon a "No, sir," answer. He said, "Son of a bitch, can't you say 'sir'?" He then began to hit and kick me and told me I had resisted arrest.

My bond was set at $400. I remained in jail until Monday, September 2, 1963. I was fined $16 for not having a job (vagrancy) and have not been tried on the charge for which I was arrested yet. I am asking the NAACP and the Department of Justice to investigate this violation of my civil rights.

SIGNED: *Percy Lee Atkins*

AMITE COUNTY

I was born in Liberty, in Amite County, Mississippi, October 8, 1922. I went to school in Liberty through the 7th grade. My father and mother, Jim and Etta Taplin, were born and raised in Amite County. They had eleven children, six girls and five boys. Three of my brothers have died. My mother and father left Liberty in 1949 to come to Baton Rouge to live.

Lewis Allen was born April 25, 1919, in Amite County and went to the 7th grade in Amite County. His father and mother, Crawford and Anner Allen, were born and raised in Amite County and had eight children, four boys and four girls. His mother died a week before he was killed, and his father left Amite County the day of his funeral.

I married Lewis, March 8, 1941. We had four children. Tommy Lewis was born August 30, 1941. Doris Etta was born January 29, 1943. Henry Crawford was born March 4, 1945. Mary Elizabeth was born September 2, 1960. Tommy finished high school in Liberty and worked for his father, logging. Doris Etta died March 8, 1957. She had epileptic spells. Henry dropped out of school in November, 1963, when his father was put in jail. He was in the 12th grade.

He says he wants to go back and finish high school and then take the trade that his daddy wanted him to take. The baby stays with me.

Lewis always logged. Before he went in the army he logged for Lloyd Cain, who lives out from Liberty. He was coming from Lloyd's house when he was killed. He was out at Lloyd's house when the call came for him to go to the army. Him and his brother both, Morris Allen, were called the same day, January 19, 1943. He served 19 months and came out August, 1944. He served in New Guinea. He took sick with a bad heart and an ulcerated stomach and they shipped him back to Springfield, Missouri, then to Alexander, Louisiana. He was discharged from there. After he came from the service, we stayed with my mommy and daddy. I went to live with my mommy and daddy when Lewis went in the army. When he came back, we stayed with them all that fall. In January, Mommy and Daddy moved out to a house in Liberty and we still stayed in the old house. We made one crop there and then we moved to a new house on the same place—it was Charlie-boy Dickson's place. The first year Lewis came back he farmed. The second year he went to the veterans' school in McComb to study mechanics. It seemed like he went to school two years.

When he stopped school he started logging for Roy Newman. He had been logging some for Jewel Spearman, while he was farming and going to school. But Jewel broke his back and Lewis took to logging for Roy Newman. We stayed on Charlie-boy's place until a year or more before we bought our own place. We bought this place from P. N. Wilson. We paid $40 a month, $200 down. He gave us two or three years to pay. We put the money in a Liberty bank and he would pick it up from New Orleans. He was a white man and Mr. Joe Gordon was our lawyer.

Mr. Gordon was always Lewis's lawyer. He arranged for Lewis's daughter to marry T. B. Allen (not related). Lewis had one child before he was married, Elaine Allen. Her grandmother raised her. Her mother stayed up in the Delta. Elaine first married Jack Carrol. She was only twelve years old and Lewis did not want her to get married. She stayed with her husband two years. When she left him, she come stayed with us until she was grown. She married T. B. Allen when she was 18, but they both had to get divorces. The lawyer came and told them they could not stay together until they got their divorces.

Then Mr. Joe Gordon fixed up some papers and told Elaine she would have to go to New Orleans and get her husband to sign them. Lewis went down to New Orleans and got Jack to sign the papers. Then they got married again.

When we finished paying for the land, Lewis borrowed some money for some logging equipment and logged for himself. We borrowed the money from the Liberty bank. The notes were $40 a month. When they began foreclosing so many people in Liberty, Negroes that is, we took it out of the bank and put it in Melvin Blaelock's name. We lost our insurance when we did this and last year we put it back in with the bank. But Lewis heard something before he decided to leave Amite for good, which made him put the property back in Melvin Blaelock's name the day he was killed. I still owe $400 and some more on the notes.

We never had any trouble with the community or the laws until Lewis testified at the trial about Herbert Lee's killing. Herbert Lee was killed on September 30th, 1961. That same day Lewis came home and said that they wanted him to testify that Herbert Lee had a piece of iron. Lewis said that Herbert Lee didn't have no iron. But he said for his family and his life he had to tell that he had an iron. Lewis told me he didn't want to tell no story about the dead, because he couldn't ask them for forgiveness. They had two courts about Herbert Lee's killing. When they had the second court Lewis did not want to testify. He said he didn't want to go back and testify no more that a man had a piece of iron when he didn't have it, but he said he didn't have no choice, he was there and he had to go to court. He said he told the FBI the truth, that Herbert Lee didn't have a piece of iron when he was shot.

After this he began to have trouble. He sold his pine logs to the Mabrys up above Liberty, had been doing it pretty near since he had been logging. They told him he could only haul two and then one load a week. Then they stopped letting him have money to buy a strip of timber that he wanted to work. Donis Hawkins' service station and Daryl Blaelock's station cut out his credit.

Then on Saturday night, late in June, we went to town to do the groceries. We parked the car across the street from the jailhouse. We was coming out from the store and someone called from across the street and I told Lewis someone called him. Lewis sent E. T. [illegible] and Doug Martin across to see what they wanted. They told them they wanted to speak to Lewis. Lewis went over to the jailhouse. They told Lewis their home was in Jackson and they wanted to call somebody out in Jackson. They gave him a note with a piece of paper, it had a phone number on it. When he came back I ask him what did the peoples want with him, he told me they wanted him to call to Jackson. We drove back home. We got back around 10 P.M. Police Officer A_____ came out about 10:30. We were watching "The Untouchables." Henry went to the door. Officer A_____ said he wanted to speak to Lewis. Lewis went outside to see what he wanted. Officer A_____ told him he was under arrest. Lewis asked him could he go his bond. Officer A_____ told him he couldn't, he had to go to jail. About that time Police Officer B_____ called and asked what was it. Officer A_____ said he was out at Lewis Allen's house and asked should he bring him in, he told him yes, bring him in. Lewis then asked Officer A_____ could he get his hat. Officer A_____ told him no. Then Lewis asked if his baby boy could go get it. When he turned to look at Henry, who was standing in the doorway, Officer A_____ struck him with a flashlight across his jaw. When Lewis turned around Police Officer C_____ throwed a gun on him and told him he better not hit that white man. They took Lewis to town and we tried to follow them.

When we got to town I saw Officer A_____ coming back from the courthouse. I asked him what did he do with Lewis; he told me he was in jail, where the hell he was going to stay. He asked me what I was doing. I told him I was going after my son Tommy. He told me to hurry up and get Tommy and get on back across the river before we all will be in jail or dead ones. Tommy went to the jailhouse Sunday to see what they had him for. His daddy told him to go tell Officer B_____ his jawbone was broke and ask him if they could get a doctor up there. Officer B_____ told Tommy he wasn't going to fool with it. Sunday evening we all decided to go to the jailhouse to see him, but Officer B_____ was at the courthouse and told us that ain't nobody told us we could go to the jailhouse and we came back home. Lewis got out on Monday. They charged him with interfering with an officer; they fined him $17.50. He went to the hospital when he got out, they told him he had a broke jawbone.

Lewis and Henry Crawford went up to Jackson to testify about this to the people up there. When they came back Henry lost his job three or four days after. He had been working at the Donis Hawkins service station. Donis told him he didn't need him no more.

That happened in the summer of 1962. One day in November of 1963, he had trouble again. Lewis had been to work and was on his way home and had stopped at Donis Hawkins' service station for gas. Police Officer A_____ was there—he spent a lot of his spare time around that service station. Officer A_____ sat there until Lewis pulled off, then stopped him and told him he was under arrest. Then reached into Lewis's glove compartment and got his pistol and carried him to jail. Tommy Lewis was with his daddy, and Officer A_____ asked him if he had a license to drive. Tommy told him yes, but he didn't have it with him because he worked in the woods and his daddy hauled the trucks. Officer A_____ told him that would be all right, for him to drive the truck on home.

I asked Tommy when he got home if he was going to do anything to see about getting his daddy out of jail. He said there wasn't anything to do until the next morning, cause they weren't going to let him out tonight. I asked him if they hit him this time, he said that he didn't think they hit him.

The next day Tommy and Henry went to the courthouse and asked Police Officer B_____ how much was their daddy's fine. He told them $500 and 90 days in jail. They went and told their daddy this and he told them to go to see if it could be all cash. They told him it would be $800 and Lewis told them to see if Mr. Barney Gray would loan them the money. But Mr. Gray told them no, he wasn't fooling with it. Then they went to Melvin Blaelock, who said he could pay the whole $800 but would rather not to. They went to more white people but they wouldn't help him no way. _____ [a local official] told them that Lewis was worth more dead than alive, just as well not get him out. Lewis told them not to try any more white people.

They had Lewis charged for a concealed weapon and a bad check. What it was, was a check for twenty some dollars he wrote to the sheriff to pay for his license tag. But he was lacking $2 or $3 in the bank to cover for it. But they never told him this, just picked him up for nothing . . . just for nothing. Well, while he was in jail they picked up a man between Gloster and Woodville and put him in jail with Lewis. This man told him they had a mob crowd to get him while he was in jail. Lewis wrote a note, put it in a matchbox and threw it down to Tommy Lewis and Henry. They went out that night and stayed around the jail. They didn't tell me cause they knew I had heart trouble. Lewis stayed in jail twenty-one days. The $800 was put up by colored people. When he got out of jail he was scared to stay at the house, he never stopped, just got all of us and came down to Baton Rouge. On the way he laid down in the car until we crossed the state line. When we crossed the line he got up and said, "Thank you, Jesus."

We stayed in Baton Rouge for a week. He called around trying to get work while he was in Baton Rouge. He went back down to Baton Rouge just before Christmas. He said he was going to try and make it through December, but he had to find him a job outside of Mississippi.

Lewis was a person like this, he mostly kept his business to himself, he wouldn't tell me things because he didn't want to worry me, I have heart trouble. But he said to me he didn't want to be in Amite County when Police Officer A_____ became _____, there would be trouble. Henry Crawford stayed out of school after his daddy got out of jail. Lewis was trying to get together to leave. He carried Henry with him everywhere he went. He let Tommy Lewis haul the logs and he stayed in the woods and he never would go to town. If he went anywhere he carried Henry with him and let him drive. Officer A_____ was elected in November and he took office in January.

On New Year's Day, [a local merchant] came out to the house. He asked me if Lewis was home. He collects the money, only we usually pay it at his [store] the first of the month. He never came out to the house before to collect. While he was talking to Lewis he told him, he say, "You see that little baby standing out by that . . . ?" Lewis told him, "Yes, sir." He say, "It would be mighty bad if she turned up burnt up, wouldn't it?" Lewis said, "Sure would." He say, "Cause she's an innocent baby but she could get burnt up just like that. I could tell you more but I'm not . . . Well, if I was you I would get my rags together in a bundle and leave here." He laughed and then started talking about the money for the bill. I think they was intending to get all of us, to burn us like they did Leo McKnight.

A week or two later Lewis walked in to the Liberty bank to pay his note—he was behind and had just carried a load of logs and when he got the money he went to the bank to pay his note. He heard E_____ and F_____, he's an old white man who has a place that joins ours, talking about him. Lewis told me he heard E_____ tell F_____ he knowed a way to foreclose Lewis out and if he did he would let F_____ have the place, you see, don't nothing separated F_____'s place from us but a fence. Lewis say they stopped talking when they saw him. Lewis paid his note and went back to the woods to work. That was two or three weeks before he was killed.

When Lewis came in from work that night, after dark, he told me what happened and said he was going to turn his place back over to Melvin Blaelock. Lewis said he was going to leave that month. He first planned to leave Saturday, January 25, but his mother took sick the Friday before. That Saturday night he went to town with his sister to see about the flowers for his mother, who was dying. While he was gone I saw some white men down at the gap. They shot, they were just shooting, then they left.

Next week on Thursday night, January 30, Lewis talked with Melvin Blaelock and told him to meet him in town Friday morning. Friday morning Lewis left the house with Henry about 8 or 9 in the morning. He was going to take the note out of the bank and put it over to Melvin and also pay the taxes on the place. He went to the bank and got things straight and then went down to Blaelock's store. Henry Crawford went to the courthouse to pay the taxes. They told him at the courthouse that Lewis would have to sign. Lewis told him to come and get me cause he didn't want to go nowhere by the courthouse.

I came into town with Henry and met Lewis at Blaelock's. We went first to T. F. Badon and signed the papers for the note. While we were at Blaelock's, Mr. Jay Butler, a Negro, came and Lewis told him he was going to leave. Jay told Lewis to come by his house and get his son's address in Chicago and if Lewis's brother didn't get him a job his son would. Then I went to the courthouse and then they drove me back home and Lewis went to work and carried a load.

Lewis came home at 12 noon that day. He eat first, then him and Henry went to Gloster to see Mr. Jewel Spearman. He told me he was going to ask him to fix out some papers for the kind of work he could do for a job when he got North. He had been telling me all the week he was planning on leaving on the 9 A.M. bus for New Orleans. Mr. Jewel wasn't there, but his son told Lewis he could fix up some papers for him. He said, "I knew your father, I remember your face"; Lewis used to log for his father. Then he asked him, he said, "What's your name," and he said Lewis Allen, then he said, "I can't fix it," and he didn't fix the papers. Then Lewis went by Jay Butler's house and got Alec's address, he is Mr. Jay's son who is over a big contracting company in Chicago. Lewis came back and told me they wouldn't fix the papers and told me to start looking for his service discharge. He cried that afternoon, he don't hardly never do nothing like that, then he went on out the house and sit down by himself for a long time cause he said he didn't want to be bothered. He said he would go that night to Mr. Lloyd Cain's, when he got home from his work. Mr. Lloyd didn't get in till night.

When he was leaving that night to go to Mr. Lloyd's to get the papers fixed he said, "I feel like I'm being watched, turn the porch light out." He had us turn the porch light out before he got into his truck. His son Henry said, "Well, Daddy, why don't you take a pistol," he says, "What good is a pistol, I put my trust in God." He went by himself cause he let Henry go to Gloster with John to a party. He told Henry to go and enjoy himself cause he didn't know when he would have another chance cause he wanted him to look after his mother and sister real good till he could send for them. He said he wouldn't be gone long, but would be back around 8:30.

I was watching TV when I heard three shots. It was around 8:30 cause "Johnny Newman," which is a Western and comes on Friday night was on. I heard the shots, I didn't know what they was, I saw the lights burning from the truck at the gap, and saw them getting dimmer and dimmer. I stayed up walking from room to room. Henry and John came back late. They found Lewis dead up under the truck. Henry went to get the sheriff, Daniel Jones.

They wouldn't let me go to the body. Daniel Jones talked to me early Saturday morning. He came back Sunday morning and told me the FBIs would come to see me, but that whatever I told them they would turn over to him cause he was investigating the case. He said they had been out to see Steptoe and he told them it was all on account of Herbert Lee's killing and Lewis's testimony, but it wasn't any use in bringing that old account up now, that I should tell the FBI the same thing I told him, not like Lewis did, telling the jury one thing and telling the FBI something else. The FBI came and talked to me Sunday night. They buried Lewis Monday. I left and came to Baton Rouge with my family the same day.

I remember Lewis walking through the house before he was killed, saying he didn't want to die, that he knew people who had been dead, died when he was a boy, that when you're dead you're dead a long time.

SIGNED: *Elizabeth Allen*

COAHOMA COUNTY

On September 1, 1963, I was arrested in the city of Clarksdale, Miss., at approximately 10:30 in the evening after I had been in an argument with James Monroe, who resides at the Cress Hotel here in Clarksdale. The argument occurred at George Black's Cafe on S. Edwards Street. During the argument no profane language was used and no punches were passed; we did, however, push each other once. After the argument was over I started home and a police car with two officers in the car stopped me and told me to get in the police car. They said, "Boy, you have been trying to dodge us." I told them, "No, sir, I have not been trying to dodge you." I was then taken to the Clarksdale City Hall.

During the questioning one of the arresting officers said, "Boy, the next time you run from me, I will take my gun and _____." Another officer said, "Atkins, didn't you hit that boy?" I said, "No, sir, I didn't hit him." He said, "You black son-of-a-bitch, when I get through with you, you are going to tell me a better lie than that." The officer then hit me with a blackjack. I threw up my arms to protect my face. On each occasion when my arms were up I was hit in the abdominal region. I was hit about six solid blows in the face and kicked in the pubic area. These blows caused my nose to start bleeding.

On the way to the cell the arresting officer gave me a paper towel and told me to wash my face. I went into the cell under my own power even though I was terrible dizzy. The beating caused the entire side of my face to swell, and for two teeth to become loosened.

Following my release on $77 bond I was examined by Dr. L. W. McCaskill, and x-rayed for a possible fracture of my jawbone at the Coahoma County Hospital. I was charged with disturbing the peace and assault and battery.

I agree to permit the NAACP and the U.S. Department of Justice to file any suits which are necessary to prevent other Negroes from being beaten in such an animal-like manner.

SIGNED: *James Atkins*

ADAMS COUNTY

I am 20 years old and a field secretary for the Student Nonviolent Coordinating Committee.

On the first of November, 1963, Bruce Payne and myself left Natchez, Mississippi, and headed north to Fayette, at about ten or ten thirty in the morning. We were distributing ballots across the southwestern portion of Mississippi for the Aaron Henry Freedom Vote. After leaving Natchez and going about two miles, I realized that we were being followed. After speeding up and slowing down the car, I realized that the car following us, a blue-green '64 Chevrolet with two male white passengers who appeared to be in their early 20s, intended to pursue us. As we proceeded north, I attempted to turn into a junction, I made a U-turn, and then, realizing that there was no mistake that the car was intending to stay with us, we continued north, speeding to attempt to lose our pursuers. After continuing for about another three miles, the car pulled up beside us and attempted to force us off the road. We were able to move to the side of the road without stopping, and continue on our way. We went on at a much higher rate of speed, with the speedometer reading about 105 m.p.h. The other car managed to catch up again and once more forced us to the side of the road. I was able to stop the car and then back up to an intersection and turn to head south. As we went south we were once more forced off the road by the same Chevrolet. We were once more able to turn around and head north. The car caught up with us again some eight or nine miles down the road, and we were forced off the road and unable to continue. The men in the other car jumped out and ran back to our car, and grabbed the door handle on the front left side of our car, but were unable to get the door open. They held a pistol and ordered us out of the car. We decided that if we were to have a chance to escape, this was it, while the two men were out of their car. As we pulled off in our car, one of the men fired the pistol into the back of the car. One shot entered the back left tire, two shots fired into the back left fender, and the fourth shot was fired into the trunk of the car. We continued at a high rate of speed north to Fayette, as the tire did not deflate. The car once more started to follow us; we turned in Fayette on a side road and were able to lose our pursuers.

SIGNED: *George Greene*

TALLAHATCHIE COUNTY

I am a Negro, 29 years of age, and live in Dutchneck, New Jersey. At the present time I am visiting my parent and have been visiting my parent, Mrs. Janie Brewer, since December, 1963, who lives in Charleston, Mississippi.

In the first week of February, 1964, my brother Charles Brewer, a friend David Baskin, and myself had been visiting some friends who live near the _____ Store in Charleston, Mississippi. We left our friends and noticed that we needed some air in one of the tires of my car. We then drove to the _____ Store to use his air pump. My brother Charles went inside the store to get some soft drinks. It seemed as if it was taking a long time for my brother Charles to come out. David Baskin walked to the door to the store, opened the door, stopped, backed away, and then turned around and started to walk real fast to the road.

I then began to hear the sound of some licks. I ran inside the store and saw my brother Charles lying on the floor. He was bleeding. He was unconscious. Mr. A_____ [the owner of the store] had backed up against the counter holding an axe handle. Another white man, Mr. B_____, was also holding an axe handle. I bent down to Charles, called him twice, and asked him, "What's the matter—what happened?" There was no response. I then pulled him up and was getting him to the door and by that time he was beginning to help himself. I then walked back to get the sunglasses that belonged to my brother. The two men had not said anything or started anything with me, so I felt that they were not going to bother me. But as soon as I started to get my sunglasses, Mr. A_____ started to cuss me, saying that I better "get him out before I kill him." Mr. A_____ then got his gun and started to shake it, when I got a blow from behind. I received a fractured skull, broken jawbone, broken nose, and a burst eyeball, with little use of my eye. However, I was able to help my brother to the car, and drive for about 40 minutes until a brother, Jesse Brewer, met me and drove my brother Charles and me to the Charleston, Miss., Hospital.

Later, about a week later, the sheriff, Alex Doghan, came and said, "Do you boys want to see me? What happened?" We told him what happened. He said that wasn't the way Mr. A_____ said it was. He then said that he was going to see Mr. A_____ and send somebody to take our story. A white man later came, who said that he was sent by the sheriff, and interviewed us. Since then, nothing has happened on our behalf.

SIGNED: _____*

*The publishers have been unable to locate the writer of this affidavit to secure his permission for its publication.

MADISON COUNTY

I am 18 years old and live in Canton, Mississippi. On February 3, 1964, Willie Galloway and I were attending a mass meeting at Pleasant Green Church in Canton. Before the meeting was over, we came out to warm up the truck we were driving. Two police officers came to the truck. (I don't know their names.) They asked Willie for his license. He told them he left it inside. They told him he'd better get it. We sat there a little while. They left to look in the church window and then came back.

They went to cussing Willie. They caught him by his collar and put a gun in his face. Then they told him to get out. They searched him and found his wallet and driver's license. They searched the truck and then told me to get out. Then they asked why did I sit there and let that boy lie to them. I told them that I only speak for myself. Then they told us both we were under arrest. Two other officers came up in a car and told us to get in. We went about a block and another police car met us. The police in the other car said, "Let us have that Galloway boy." They took him in their car and they took me to jail in the other.

They told me to sit down in the jailhouse for questioning. They wanted to know who was doing most of the talking at the meeting. They asked about George Washington and how he got his money. I told them I didn't know. There were about five officers in the jail at that time. Then one came over with a night stick and hit me on the top and side of the head about eight times and broke the stick over my head. Another stood behind my chair with a rubber hose and hit me about four or five times with it. Another had a parking meter and bumped it up against my head two or three times.

One of them got a razor and cut a bald spot through my hair. Another came up with a pistol and threatened to kill me. But one of the policemen said, "Don't kill him, I want to do it myself," and he fired two shots at my feet. One policeman stood on my foot while they were questioning me.

One policeman asked if I bought Mosby milk. I told him no, and when he asked why I didn't I told him we were boycotting Mosby milk. He said he'd give me a nickel and when I went to school I'd better buy some Mosby milk. When I told him I wouldn't do it, he hit me again until I said I would buy Mosby milk. Another got some whiskey from a cabinet like he was going to make me drink some, but one of them said, "No, don't get him drunk."

Then they told me to go home and let it soak in, and if we told anyone what happened, they'd put us in the lake. They told us if anyone asked what happened to tell them "we were just checking on the license." Then they let me go about 12:30. They said I'd have to walk home but when I went out Willie Galloway, Jr., was sitting in front of the jail. We got in the truck and went back to the church and then to the projects to pick up the girls that came in with us and went home. The next day we went to the doctor and we saw him about four or five times and lost four or five days out of school.

SIGNED: *Arthur Harris*

FORREST COUNTY

I am a 25-year-old Student Nonviolent Coordinating Committee staff worker. I have been working as a civil rights worker or attending college at Tougaloo since June, 1961. I was working in Hattiesburg on voter registration since January 7, 1964.

I was arrested on February 5, on false charges of disturbing the peace, profanity, and resisting arrest. Later, at the trial, contempt of court was added to the list of charges. Judge Lenard found me guilty and I was taken to the Forrest County Work Camp on February 6, 1964, to serve a four-month sentence plus a $391 fine.

On Monday, February 17, [a] work camp [official] had a separate cell fixed up to keep me in as punishment for not working hard enough. Just before he put me in, a prisoner, A_____, jumped on me and knocked me down. I noticed that [the camp official] was standing in the door watching. A_____ said, "Get up," which I did to show that I was not afraid. He hit me a number of times in the face, giving me a black eye and a couple of bruises. He grabbed me around the neck and attempted to gouge at my eyes with his thumbs. After a while, [the camp official] stopped the assault and locked me in the room.

On Saturday, as no one had contacted me, I called the office and told them I'd been hit. The same guard was listening as we made phone calls (allowed on Saturdays) but I went ahead and told Sandy Leigh, one of the other SNCC workers, what had happened. In the middle of the conversation [the camp official] grabbed the phone and started hitting me. He knocked me against the door, knocked me down outside, and kicked me. He then locked me back up.

On Monday, April 21, Constable B_____ came to the camp, told me to get my things, and that I was going to Jackson for trial. My case had been transferred to the federal courts by my attorneys, Mr. George Crockett and Mr. Ben Smith. As B_____ took me to the county jail, he attempted to get me into an argument by speaking derogatorily about the movement and Negroes in general. During the discussion I said that I didn't think much of a person who would arrest others just to make money and that "he was lower than many people who he arrested." B_____ became quite angry and hit me across the face with the back of his hand. Neither of us spoke the rest of the way to the jail. I put in a complaint about him to the FBI when they came to see me Wednesday.

When I got to the Hinds County Jail I was assigned to one of the cells about midway along the hall. Later [a prison official] apparently spoke to the trusties that were in the bull pen and I was moved to the cell furthermost from the entrance. While I was in the cell before lockup, a number of the prisoners gathered outside the door. I heard one prisoner tell others that the [prison official] had offered cigarettes to have me beaten up. They knew that my address was at Tougaloo, which I had told the [prison official] but none of the prisoners. They also knew that I'd been with the voter registration drive in Hattiesburg, which I wasn't about to say anything about.

Soon they came into the cell. A heavy obese man named C_____, a large muscular gray-haired man who had been in Parchman, and a young man I heard called D_____, pulled me down from the bunk. They kicked me many times in the side and kidneys, hit me with their fists all over my body, except my face as they didn't want the beating to show. The gray-haired man beat me with a wide leather strap. I didn't resist the beating because there were three of them and I thought they were looking for an excuse to hurt me worse. I just took the beating without saying much.

After lights out, the prisoner referred to as D_____ attempted to have homosexual relations with me. When I told him that I didn't do things like that, he attempted to beat me into submission. He took my belt and hit me with the leather strap. He hit me many times with his fist, tried to knock me down, and kicked me. I finally tussled with him, although I was sick, to keep him from beating me unconscious. He finally gave up and left me alone. An x-ray taken on May 23 shows that I got two broken ribs from the beating. I also had many muscle bruises.

When the writ of habeas corpus was turned down, I was driven back to the prison camp. Police Officer E_____ said he would investigate my beating, but I don't think he did. The guards at the camp saw my condition but wouldn't get a doctor. The next day, A. C. Butler took me to Dr. Graves. Graves said that I had no broken bones or internal injuries, and gave me four pills.

On May 21, while we were working on the McCullen Bridge, [the camp official] walked over to me and unexpectedly hit me across the face with his hands. He claimed I wasn't working fast enough. Robert Nailer, Joe Bradly Nix, Julius Harris, James Barnes, Bob Moss, and the other guard, Hubert Sholar, were witnesses to the fact that [the camp official] struck me without any provocation. That evening I was taken back to the jail. After an hour or so in the jail, [Police Officer E_____] said my fine had been paid and he released me.

SIGNED: *Peter Stoner*

HINDS COUNTY

My home is in New York, New York. I have been in Mississippi working for CORE (the Congress of Racial Equality) since mid-January, 1964. During the period from mid-January to the end of March, I was working in Canton on voter registration. On Monday, March 30, 1964, I left the COFO (Council of Federated Organizations) office at 1017 Lynch Street, Jackson, at about 6:30 P.M. and went out to eat dinner. I went with another worker, Miss Helen O'Neal. We went to a place up the street, called Smackover's, where we sat and had a leisurely dinner, including several cups of coffee. Neither of us had any sort of alcoholic beverage before, during, or after the meal.

After the meal was over, we went across the street to a drug store, where each of us bought one or two personal items such as a toothbrush, pencils, filling a prescription, and the like. We were in the drugstore for approximately fifteen minutes.

We left the drug store and started to walk back to the COFO office. We were walking side by side on the sidewalk. We were on the north side of Lynch Street and were walking east. By this time it was dark outside, and the time was approximately 7:30 or 7:45 P.M. Just after walking by the Masonic Temple at 1072 Lynch Street, we passed by a police prisoner van. Parked just behind the van was a police car with four policemen sitting inside. We walked by the car, glancing inside but not stopping or paying special attention to it.

After we had walked perhaps twenty steps beyond the police car, we heard a call of "Hey!" behind us. We turned around and started back when one of the officers motioned to us. As we reached the officer who had called us (he was out of the car and standing on the sidewalk; all of the other officers remained in the car), the officer asked me what I had been drinking. I replied, "Nothing." The officer said something like, "Nonsense," and then, "Come along with me." I gave a package I was carrying to Miss O'Neal, who then walked off towards the COFO office.

The officer opened up the back door of the police prisoner van, a sort of panel truck with wire mesh across the windows in back and benches on both sides and in the front of the back compartment. I climbed in and sat down on one of the side benches. The back door was then closed behind me and locked with a padlock on the outside. Two officers climbed in the front seat of the van; I could see them through a mesh-covered window that looked through from my compartment into the front seat of the van. The van was then driven to the Jackson police station, the police car following close behind. Once or twice the van stopped short for no apparent reason, and I was thrown towards the front of the compartment. I learned to hold tight to the bench to prevent anything serious from happening.

When the two vehicles reached the basement of the city jail, the padlock was unlocked and I stepped down and started to walk with the officers towards the elevator. Inside the elevator the light was switched off by the officer pressing the buttons for the floors. The light was not turned on again until we reached the floor towards which we were headed.

When we reached the room where I was booked, I was asked to stand in front of a desk on which there were two typewriters. A form was inserted into one of the typewriters, and a series of questions were asked me. These questions—name, address, name of mother, name of father, date of birth, and the like—were the same questions asked of me when I had previously entered the Jackson City Jail, so I believe the questions were all part of the form.

After the form had been completed, the officers started asking other questions. They asked who I worked for, how much money I made, when I got paid—all of which I answered. They then asked what my wife thought of my dating a Negro girl—which I did not answer. They asked several other questions which I do not remember; then they asked if I would deny if I was a Communist. I said that my political beliefs were not pertinent to the charges being placed against me and that I would not answer any questions about my political beliefs. Right after this one of the officers started to hit me.

The officer was standing behind me. We had moved to a desk on another side of the room, where my pockets had been emptied and several questions had been asked about the contents of my pockets. Comments were made about how much money I had (about $20) and about a sheet of paper—very old and crinkled—with "The Movement" written across the top and a list of names on it. The officers at one point had asked how long I had been here and I had replied two months. One of the officers said he didn't believe me, that he had ridden up and down Lynch Street many times but had never seen me. After this business with the pockets we had moved back to the desk with the typewriters, and the officers were arranged with two behind me and two in front of me.

The officer who began to hit me was standing behind me. He raised his arm and came down with the side of his hand across my neck. He repeated this motion about half a dozen times, each time striking hard. I gave under each blow but straightened up for the succeeding one. As he hit me the first time, he said something like "nigger-lover," but said nothing for each of the other blows.

After these blows, the officer turned me slightly towards him and started to hit me in the body and stomach and face with his fists. As he did this, he forced me back the six or eight feet across the room until I was against the wall. He then took my head in one of his hands and slammed my head against the wall two or three times. After this, he pulled me forward and forced me to the ground. While I was on the ground he kicked me several times in the stomach and chest.

I then got up, and he started hitting me on the body again with his fists. He also kicked up with his leg several times and kicked me in the stomach. After this, he walked into one of the other rooms off the booking room.

At one point another officer joined in the hitting, but he did very little. The two remaining officers simply looked on the whole time.

The officer who had administered most of the beating came back out of the side room very soon. He was breathing very hard. At this point the officers looked at me and mumbled something about resisting arrest and nodded to each other. I had resumed my position in front of the table with the typewriters. As the officer who had done the hitting typed out something

I noticed his name plate; it read _____. I did not notice the names of any of the other officers.

I would estimate that the whole beating took from 30 to 45 seconds.

Shortly after this, the jailer came into the room and led me off to my cell. I was kept by myself in one of the investigation cells overlooking the Hinds County Courthouse.

Several of the trusties (Negro) who serviced the cell spoke to me during the next two days that I was there. They asked if I were the fellow who was beaten in the booking room on Monday night. When I replied that I was, they asked why. I said that I was a civil rights worker. Several of the people told me in turn about how they had been beaten when they had come in.

At my trial my lawyer, Mr. Jess Brown, spoke with the prosecuting attorney. I pleaded *nolo contendere,* and fines against me of $15 on one count, $25 on another count, and 30 days suspended sentence on the third count were levied. The three counts were drunkenness and resisting arrest, the suspended sentence for vagrancy; but there was a mixup at the trial and I do not know.

I served two days in the county jail before money came to pay my fines and release me.

SIGNED: *Richard A. Jewett*

ADAMS COUNTY

I do solemnly swear that the below information is true, concerning me and some of the members of the Natchez Police Department in which I recognized one officer A_____, who attacked me physically without any cause to my knowledge, on Tuesday, May 19, 1964. The incident happened approximately 9 o'clock A.M. on Concord Street just before crossing the railroad track coming north about a city block and one half from my home.

When the officer on the motorcycle first blew the siren, I could not stop immediately due to the oncoming traffic, but proceeded to stop, putting my left arm out of the 1956 Ford pick-up truck that I was driving. After stopping, I stepped from the truck with both hands up. The officer then told me to place both hands on top of the truck, informing me at the same time that I was under arrest. I asked him, "For what?" Then he began beating me across the head with his night stick. After having knocked me down, he hit me in the left side of the face even with my left ear. The officer called in for several squad cars. Then the officers took me to jail.

After having gotten me to jail, several officers beat me and dragged me around in jail, kicking and beating me all at the same time. One officer picked up one of my legs and another took the other leg and proceeded to drag me and pull me apart.

While in jail (after having been beaten terribly) I asked for a doctor, but the officers refused to call one.

I was not able to contact a doctor until Thursday, May 21, 1964, about 10 o'clock A.M. The doctor stated my skull was fractured and jawbone broken.

I also recognized Lieutenant [Police Officer B_____] when officers were beating me, and I asked him to please make them stop beating me, but he did not answer. The desk officer, who took my package (billfolder with $1.13 in it, driver's license, one statement for a doctor bill, papers of identification, and one small pocketknife), asked the other officers to stop beating me, but they did not.

After this, all I remember is waking up in a jail cell. I asked a Negro man (who was a trusty) to ask the officer to take me to a doctor because I was bleeding so badly. They would not.

I am 54 years of age and was born in Natchez, Mississippi. I do solemnly swear that this information is true to the best of my knowledge.

SIGNED: _____*

*The publishers have been unable to locate the writer of this affidavit to secure his permission for its publication.

HINDS COUNTY

I reside in New York, N.Y. I have been in Mississippi since January, 1964, working on voter registration.

On the evening of May 24, 1964, I went with Euvester Simpson, Doris Derby, and Dona Moses, all Negro SNCC workers, to the Alamo Theater on North Farish Street in Jackson. We attended a double feature starting at about 8:30 P.M. After the movie was over, at about 1 A.M., the morning of May 25, 1964, someone (I think it was Dona Moses) called the COFO office at 1017 Lynch Street to see if there was a possibility of a ride back from the movies. There was no car available, so we decided to take a taxi.

The four of us walked up the street to the Dotty Cab Company. Several ladies were in the dispatching booth. We asked if we could get a cab; they said there were no cabs at the office but that they would call one in on the radio. We stood outside the cab office to wait. At some point after about five minutes of waiting, Miss Derby remembered that she had left some of her things in the movie house, so she and Miss Simpson walked back to the theater to pick the things up.

While Mrs. Moses and I stood waiting outside the cab stand, a police van pulled up in the cab lot. The officer in the driver's seat, who I later learned was named A_____, called to me to come over. I went over to the van, and as I drew near the van Officer A_____ said something like, "What's that on your breath?" or "What have you been drinking?" I replied, "Nothing." I had had no alcoholic beverages of any kind to drink at any time during the day or evening. Officer A_____ got out of the driver's seat and said I was under arrest. We both went around to the back of the police van. The back door was opened, and I climbed inside; the door was shut behind me. As the van got under way one of the officers closed the panel which separates the front seat from the benches in the back of the van. We drove directly to the Jackson police station.

At the station, the van drove into the basement and stopped. The back door of the van was opened and I got out. The two officers and I walked together to the elevator. We got inside the elevator and the outside door of the elevator was closed. The light in the elevator was on. Officer A_____ immediately started to hit me. He struck me blows on the face and on the body with his fists. As he hit me he said something like, "You dirty _____, calling the FBI," and "You _____ Communist."

At one point I was forced down on my haunches, and Officer A_____ struck out with his feet trying to kick me; I warded off his feet. Later I was forced against the back wall, and I felt a metal object against my neck. Officer A_____ said something like, "This ought to teach you." I presume the metal object was a gun. I was given many punches on the back of my neck with the side of Officer A_____'s hand. These were interspersed among the other blows. Several times Officer A_____ struck out with his knee to try to knee me in the groin.

The other officer held me a little, but he did little if any of the beating. I would estimate that the total beating took about 30 seconds.

After the beating was finished, the elevator went up to the second floor. I was booked in a room with the two officers who arrested me and with a third officer who was wearing a white shirt. The usual personal information form was filled out by Officer A_____. It was at this point that I determined the officer's name by reading A_____ on his name plate. The only unusual event in filling out the form was when the officer asked for my occupation; without waiting for me to answer, he said "None" and wrote a short word like none on the form. I said that I worked for the Congress of Racial Equality, but he made no notice that he heard me.

I was taken to a cell that is usually referred to as the drunk tank. It is a large room with stone shelves around the edges, these shelves being used for sitting and sleeping. In one corner of the room is a hole in the floor; this hole is used for waste. After I was in the tank for a while, I heard a voice at the door call "Jewett." I went to the door, and there were Officer A_____ and about five other officers. Officer A_____ held the door open and said, "I just wanted you to meet the sergeant." He motioned to a man with stripes on his arms; this man's name plate read B_____. Sergeant B_____ asked routine questions such as how long had I been in Jackson, how long had I been working for CORE, what sort of work did I do, and did I have a family. I answered all these questions.

Sergeant B_____ then asked, "Have any of your rights been violated?" I replied that I'd prefer not to answer that question. Officer A_____ then asked two questions, the sense of which was to ask whether I was a Communist or whether I was a Communist sympathizer. I said that I'd prefer not to answer the questions. I was then returned to the cell.

About 6 A.M., I was moved from the drunk tank to a private cell of my own on the back of the second floor.

At my trial on May 25, 1964, I was represented by counsel, Mr. Carsie Hall. There were initially two charges against me—vagrancy and drunkenness. The vagrancy charge was dropped, and a $15 bond for the drunkenness charge was posted.

At no time during the events related above did I strike out at the officers or attempt to run from them.

SIGNED: *Richard A. Jewett*

MADISON COUNTY

On 5-29-64, I left the Freedom House at 838 Lutz Street, Canton, at 9:00 A.M. and went to Mount Zion Church. From Mount Zion Church I went with five other people to Asbury Church. On the way, Canton policemen stopped and asked me for my driver's license and asked the other five people for identification. One of the officers said to me: "So you want to be a smart nigger."

Joe Lee Watts and myself, at Mount Zion Church later on, were sitting on the lawn and singing freedom songs. One of the officers who had stopped me earlier came up to us and spoke to me: "If I had my own way with you, I'd whip you." He and another officer asked me if I wanted to fight. I told them that I didn't want to fight. The officer then said: "You're so bad, nigger. Come on and fight me." Then he asked me why I was singing freedom songs. He turned around. Someone else said something. The officers thought it was me who had spoken. They dragged me to the street. They both grabbed me—one by each arm. One of them beat me with a stick and knocked me out. I had seen about eight men coming toward me; then I lost consciousness. When I came to, I was lying on the concrete in the fire department. Then they called an ambulance. I stayed in the hospital for about an hour. The doctor said that I was too sick to go to jail, but they took me to the county jail anyway.

When I was getting out of the car at the county jail, one of the officers chopped me on the front of the neck. Another officer twisted my arm. One said: "Nigger, why are you looking up in the sky? It's not the end of the world yet."

On May 30, 1964, at about 7 A.M. a city policeman came to the county jail and took my fingerprints. While he was fingerprinting me, he asked me something. I didn't say "Yes, sir," so another policeman slapped me down, on my head where I had been beaten on the preceding day. The second policeman said to the first: "When you get through fingerprinting him, I'm going to take him in the other room and teach him a lesson—not to fight white folks." He took me into the room and hit me twelve or thirteen times on my head in the same place; every time that he hit me he would say: "I'm going to teach you not to fight white folks." When he finished, he gave me his handkerchief to wipe the blood, and he told me not to tell anyone what he had done to me or he would throw me in the river.

SIGNED: *McKinley Hamblin*

MADISON COUNTY

On Saturday, May 30, at 4 P.M. I contacted Hamid Kisselbasch at his home in Tougaloo, Mississippi. Kisselbasch, who was assistant professor in social sciences at Tougaloo College, is a Pakistani who said he has been in the United States as a student and teacher since 1959, and an assistant professor at Tougaloo since September, 1963.

Kisselbasch told me that on Friday, May 29, he was in Canton with the Rev. R. Edwin King, King's wife, and two white Tougaloo College students, attending a meeting at a Negro church. He told me they left by car, with himself driving, before 9 P.M. and that at the intersection of Highway 51 and Interstate 55 they were forced off the road by a car which had been following them out of town. Before leaving Canton, he added, white men carrying sticks were conferring with uniformed police officers. Kisselbasch told me that after his car was forced off the road, other vehicles pulled up, and a group of white men surrounded the car. All car doors were locked, but the driver's window was open, and one of the group of white men reached through the window and opened the driver's door, Kisselbasch said. He told me his assailant pulled him halfway out of the car—Kisselbasch said he clung to the steering wheel—and administered two hard cracks with a stick resembling a baseball bat on his (Kisselbasch's) head. Then the assailant tore Kisselbasch's shirt and pulled Kisselbasch's necktie tight around his neck, Kisselbasch said. There followed a third blow with the stick, a relatively light one to Kisselbasch's forehead, Kisselbasch said. Throughout the attack, Kisselbasch said, the assailant and his companions cursed and threatened those in the Tougaloo party. Kisselbasch said he bled, but not profusely.

Kisselbasch said one of the attackers said, "Let's have a party and fix these nigger-lovers so they never come back to Canton." Another member of the attacking group decided to let Kisselbasch & Co. proceed, however. Kisselbasch drove back to Jackson, he said, and they were followed to within two blocks of the Governor's Mansion. He said they stopped at the Mansion and asked to see the governor, but were refused permission to see him. They also stopped at the highway patrol, Kisselbasch said, but the officers there showed scant interest in the attack and concentrated their questioning on the Negro meeting in Canton.

When I talked with Kisselbasch on May 30, he complained of headaches and a sore throat from the necktie being twisted around his neck. He said he had contacted the Pakistani Embassy in Washington that morning, and that the ambassador had promised to take action. Kisselbasch had these comments: "When these things happen, and law authorities take no action, it leaves the individual practically helpless. Last night I came to realize at first hand what I had often heard before about police treatment of civil rights workers: that there are individuals here who are capable of carrying out their threats, and that their intentions are dangerous, and somehow subhuman.

"The most dangerous aspect is that there appears to be no recourse to law. I am worried about this society and hope that violence will not be able to continue unchecked, especially since the struggle which is now going on is so important."

SIGNED: *David P. Welsh*

HINDS COUNTY

Around the supper hour on February 3, 1964, I was sitting in the COFO office at 1017 Lynch Street in Jackson when Joyce Ladner phoned to ask what was going on at Jackson State College. Minutes later, someone, possibly Clifford Vaughs, came into the office saying that there was a demonstration going on at Jackson State. He was then followed by Kirksey, who brought in the same news.

I went up to Dalton and Lynch Streets with Willie Blue. There were roughly 100–200 persons standing on three of the four corners with about 8 policemen standing in the intersection directing traffic. Suddenly, from out of nowhere, came the roar of engines. Twelve to fifteen motorcycles were coming up Lynch in formation—single file. They drove up Lynch, passed Dalton (going west), and lined up width-wise along Lynch. The policemen then dismounted.

Charles Cobb came over and told me what had happened: a girl student from Jackson State had been hit by a speeding car on Lynch Street while she was in a pedestrian crosswalk. The students who saw this became incensed because it seemed to them that the police let the driver go without even taking his name. The students then held a rally on campus and eventually the Jackson Negro policemen were sent on campus to "investigate" matters. Finally, the campus area was closed to "outsiders" and people started gathering at Lynch and Dalton primarily to see what was wrong more than anything else.

While Cobb and I stood there talking, at least another 100 people had gathered on three of the four corners that made up the intersection. The police occupied the fourth corner and were not allowing anyone now to go west on Lynch Street past Dalton unless the person was a student.

Barricades were placed across Lynch and cars couldn't even go west on Lynch past Dalton now. Finally a voice cried, "Disperse them." Utilizing a wedge-type formation, the police completely cleared the three corners of people in a matter of seconds. Cobb and I returned to the office.

A fellow entered the office with a gash over his eye that required 17 stitches. He was from Utica College and was in Jackson to attend the Jackson State game with some other school. He had been blocked by the police from going to the auditorium where the game was to be held.

After the game, a group of students demonstrated in the crosswalk, walking back and forth. Charles Evers appeared on the scene and asked the students to return to their dorms, that the police chief had promised them a light [a traffic light], and that there was no need to protest. Before he could finish, a line of police, spread from sidewalk to sidewalk, were coming down Lynch toward the students, all with rifles in their arms.

Suddenly, a bottle crashed in front of one of them, then another. The police then reacted by shooting in the air. Students screamed and scattered everywhere. The police were still shooting, but now the muzzles of the weapons were parallel to the ground. Emma and I went into the Penguin Cafe. Some 15 to 20 minutes later, between 6 and 8 policemen entered the cafe and told those of us in there to leave, saying, "This place is closed for the night." As we were going down Lynch, shots rang out continuously.

Just as we passed Smackover's, I was shot in the arm. I told Emma I had been hit and she led me up a little alley where we went to a house with a phone and she called the office. She told Cobb what had happened and Charlie said that George Greene had been shot in the chest. On hearing this, we forgot all about my arm and hurried back to the office. An ambulance was in front of the office taking away a fellow who had been shot in the buttocks. George was apparently O.K.—his eyeglasses case had stopped the bullet.

The office was now filled with pressmen who were writing stories. I had Cliff take me to the University Hospital, where the bullet was removed from my arm. I was then taken to the police station, where I signed a statement about what had happened.

SIGNED: *Jesse T. Morris*

PIKE COUNTY

On June 8, 1964, I, _____, and two friends, Andre Martinsons and Rene Jonas, were driving on U.S. 51 from New Orleans toward Jackson when we stopped for lunch in McComb, Mississippi. No sooner had I parked my car, a 1964 Volkswagen with Massachusetts license plates, in the lot of a drive-in restaurant than a police car with two McComb officers inside drove into the lot, surveyed us closely, noted the license number of my car, and drove out, parking across the street. A few minutes later, an unmarked car drove into the lot and a man dressed in plain clothes approached us, showing his badge and identifying himself as Mr. Guy, Chief of Police of the town of McComb. He asked us what we were doing in McComb. He inquired if we had any business being in McComb and he suggested if we had no business that we keep moving and leave the town as soon as possible. Mr. Martinsons informed the police chief that we were on a two-week vacation riding through the South and that we had connections with several magazines who were interested in any articles we might write about the situation in the South. Mr. Martinsons told the chief that we were just passing through McComb on our way to Jackson and were calling a few citizens of the town on our way through. Since the officials of the town of McComb seemed so interested in us however, Mr. Martinsons asked if we could interview the mayor of the town. Mr. Guy said the mayor was always free and directed us to the city hall.

We interviewed the mayor of McComb, a Mr. Burt, I believe, for several hours, between 2–4 P.M. in his office at city hall. He explained that McComb was a quiet town with few internal problems. Whatever trouble there was, he said, was caused by "Northern agitators," among whom he classed the Justices of the Supreme Court, civil rights workers, and newspaper reporters. The mayor recounted one incident of reporters being thrown through a plate glass window in the center of town in 1961, but was quick to add that no such thing would probably happen to us; we seemed like such "nice fellows." After leaving the mayor's office, we interviewed the police chief, Mr. Guy, for several minutes. He also felt that there was little internal trouble in

McComb and boasted of his police force consisting of 16 full-time officers and 25 volunteers, all of whom were legally deputized and armed, although they wore no uniforms. He was quite proud of their capabilities and boasted that they were "riot-trained by the FBI." Mr. Jonas stated that since he had such an able police force he felt that our civil liberties would be adequately protected during the few hours more we chose to remain in McComb.

We left city hall at about 4:30 P.M. and drove across town to the Negro section of the city. For the next 4 or 5 hours we talked to various members of the Negro community. Many of them were reluctant to speak to us because wherever we went in the town we were followed quite obviously by either the chief of police in his private car, by two police officers in a cruiser, or by a white man in an unmarked car. The police chief never spoke to us but he never tried to hide the fact that he was keeping us and the people to whom we spoke under close surveillance. Several times he would have just left the home of a person we were planning to speak to. At our last stop, the home of a Negro civil rights leader whose business establishment had been bombed the week before, police cars patrolled by the house on the average of once every 10 minutes the two hours we were there. The Negro citizens of McComb we spoke to gave us quite another picture of the city from the one that the public officials had presented. They warned us that the Klan had been substantially re-activated in that area during the past 6 months and one informant said that the mayor of the town, Mr. Burt, was himself a past president of the White Citizens Council.

At approximately 9 P.M. that evening we left the home of this Negro civil rights leader and drove through the center of McComb, following U.S. 51 toward Jackson. We were followed out of the city by a McComb police cruiser that kept about 30 yards behind my car all the way despite the fact that I was going 10 miles below the registered speed limit. At one stoplight I could see from my rear view mirror an unmarked car pull parallel to the police cruiser, idle beside it, and then follow it as it followed us out of the city. At the city limits the cruiser turned off the road and headed back toward the town of McComb. The unmarked car continued to follow us.

Three to five miles outside the city, after a stretch of gravel road, this unmarked car passed my Volkswagen and started to slow down. As I tried to pass it on the highway, it weaved in front of me. The lights in the rear seat were turned on, revealing two men in the front seat and two men in the back. One man in the back seat pointed a revolver at me (I was driving the car) and motioned for us to stop. At that same time I noticed for the first time that a second car had pulled up behind me and was trailing my rear bumper. A third car pulled up beside me at this point, forcing my Volkswagen off the road. A man jumped from this car and yelled, "This is the law." I do not know whether he meant that he was vigilante law or that he was one of the un-uniformed auxiliary police force of McComb. Before we could see whether he carried a badge or not, somewhere between 6 and 8 white men jumped from the other two cars, several of them carrying rifles and revolvers, shouting "You Northern agitators are going to get it now," "This is it, Yankee," etc. They surrounded my car, and one man, the one who had pointed the revolver at me from the rear seat of the car in front of me, came up to my window, pointed the gun at my head, and ordered me out of the car. As he pushed me toward the underbrush, I could see a man (I later found out he was wearing brass knuckles) beginning to beat my friends in the car.

The man who held the gun on me was wild-eyed and seemed strangely scared. He demanded to know what I was doing in McComb. I repeated the story we had told the chief of police. He asked why we "Northern agitators" continued to come down here. I tried to explain that we were not "Northern agitators" and that those who did come down to Mississippi to uphold civil rights were not down here for a vacation; they were brave individuals who expected to be beaten by private individuals, vigilantes, auxiliary police, call them what you will. He then demanded what I was doing in "niggertown," what "niggers" I had spoken to. I stated that he knew this as well as I did since the chief of police had followed us everywhere we went, taking names. He did not push the point.

Meanwhile several cars and trucks passed along U.S. 51 heading to and from McComb; while they slowed to gaze at the cars parked in the middle of the road, none of them stopped. Our attackers began to get frightened, however, that someone might recognize them or call for help. They jumped into their cars and driving without lights headed back toward McComb.

I returned to my car and drove my friends into Jackson. We were wary of being treated in the white municipal hospital and called the COFO office for assistance. They contacted a Negro doctor, who aided my friends. Mr. Jonas required about 30 stitches for lacerations on his face and head; Mr. Martinsons needed 8 stitches for a deep gash on his head. That same evening, 12:10 A.M., June 9, I telephoned Chief Guy and registered an official complaint. He did not seem surprised that we had been ambushed.

The next morning, June 9, my parents protested to their State Senator, Edward Kennedy, and Mr. Jonas called his Senator, Javits, for assistance. We also registered official complaints to the U.S. Attorney in Jackson, requesting prosecution of the officials of McComb, and to the U.S. marshal, stating that no U.S. citizen upholding the Constitution was safe in Mississippi and demanding federal protection. The FBI interviewed us next. When they discovered that the Jackson police were harassing us and that the police chief of McComb had wired a description of my car across the state, they suggested that we leave Mississippi as soon as possible. They too reiterated that they could offer us no protection; but they said that we should call them a half-hour after leaving Jackson (since many phones in the city are tapped), tell them what route we had taken out of the city, and call them at frequent intervals thereafter so that if we were missing, they would have some idea where to find us or our bodies. We left Jackson the following morning, June 10, following the route through Meridian, and two hours later were out of the State of Mississippi.

SIGNED: _____*

*The publishers have been unable to locate the writer of this affidavit to secure his permission for its publication.

LOWNDES COUNTY

I am 18 years old and live in Ruleville, Mississippi. On the afternoon of June 8th, 1964, Charles McLaurin and I started out from Ruleville. In Greenwood, Miss., we picked up Sam Block, Willie Peacock, James Jones. Our destination was Atlanta, Georgia, where we were to attend a meeting of the SNCC staff.

Between Mayhew Junction and Starkville we were followed by a '56 Mercury. The car pulled up behind us and cut his lights off, then pulled out like he was going to pass and then didn't pass. We slowed down at that point. At Mayhew Junction he turned off. At the intersection of Rt. 45 and 82 the highway patrol pulled up behind us and pulled us off the road. Officer A_____, the highway patrolman, said to us: "You god-damn niggers want to change our way of life." He then told me (I was driving at the time) to get out of the car. Then he told the others to get out on the other side of the car and stand by our car. Then he searched the car. He then went to call Officer B_____ and told Officer B_____ to pick us up cause we were "god-damn niggers trying to change our way of life." Then we were searched one by one. By this time Officer B_____ had arrived.

Officer B_____ handcuffed all of the others, but not me. Then he told me to pick up all the literature in a box and put it in the back of his car. (The literature was Mrs. Hamer's campaign literature and Summer Project brochures.) After I put the literature in the back of his car he told me to get in the back of his car (a '63 white Ford). He told me he was going to take me to the courthouse but before he took me to the courthouse he took me out of the car; I refused to get out. So he pulled me out. He started hitting me with his fists and after about twenty blows he got his blackjack out and hit me one time with it and knocked me down. Then he told me to get back in the car. While he was beating me he asked me if any white folks had ever treated me bad; I told him yes and he hit me again. He asked me again had any white folks in Mississippi treated me bad and I told him no. At that point he helped me back into the car. Then he took me to the county jail (Lowndes) where I was questioned by Officer B_____. He asked for my driver's license and to take everything out of my pockets. Then he told me to step back and told the others to do the same, i.e., to take stuff out of their pockets and step back. Then we were taken into a cell; there was only one cell in the jail so we were all together; a girl and three other boys besides us were all together in the cell. In about 5 minutes I was called again to be questioned and was taken to Officer B_____'s office. I had a friend's ID card in my pocket and he asked me if my friend was a Negro or a nigger. I told him a Negro. The same highway patrolman was there and took out his blackjack and again asked if my friend was a Negro or a nigger. He started to hit me with the blackjack and I told him my friend was a nigger.

Then I was taken back to the jail; 5 minutes later Officer C_____ came to take one of the other guys out. He took Sam Block to Officer B_____'s office, asked him a few questions, and beat him up. Then Officer C_____ brought Sam back and took James Jones out. Then he brought James back and took Willie Peacock out. Then he brought Willie Peacock back and took Charles McLaurin out. In each case they were beaten right in Officer B_____'s office.

We were kept in jail overnight and the next morning about 10 A.M. we were taken down to the city police department and fingerprinted and photographed and interviewed again. We were asked names, addresses, and phone numbers and asked where did we work. I am a day laborer and told him so. Then we were taken to the court; the presiding judge was Judge _____. I was charged with reckless driving. We were going about 35 miles an hour when the incident occurred. He said I was in the wrong lane, which is untrue. I was also charged with running two stop signs, which was false. After this the judge told me to sit down and that my trial, the State of Mississippi vs. James Black, would begin. I was asked questions then such as: "Were you encouraged to drive the car." I told him no. I told him I was a day laborer. "Are you on the NAACP staff?" I told him no. "Do you belong to any organization?" I told him no. Then he told me to sit down again and called in the other boys one by one. Then they were asked the same questions: Were they on the SNCC payroll. They answered yes. Then we were all told to go out while they had a conference in the courtroom. About five minutes later I was called back alone. Then I was told that he was going to let me off light providing I would leave town and never return. He charged me $5 for running each stop sign and $2 for driver education and charged the other four $4 each for the night they spent in jail. The reason he didn't charge me the $4 fee was because I had been officially arrested. We were then taken back to the jail and given our personal belongings. After which we paid the fine and a city policeman drove us to the filling station where the car was. We were charged $2.08 for storage. Then we continued our trip to Atlanta.

Officer A_____, the highway patrolman, has a badge number _____, and his license tag number was _____. We were followed between Mayhew Junction and Starkville between 10 and 10:30 P.M. and were stopped by the highway patrolman at about 10:30 P.M.

SIGNED: *James Charles Black*

NESHOBA COUNTY

I am 22 years old and the wife of Michael H. Schwerner, one of the three civil rights workers who have been missing in or near Philadelphia, Miss., since June 21, 1964. Michael and I came to Mississippi on about January 16 this year as field staff workers for the Congress of Racial Equality, assigned to the Council of Federated Organizations. On about January 21 we went to Meridian, Mississippi, with the purpose of establishing a community center in that city which would provide such services which the state and local authorities would not provide for Negro citizens. From that time until June 21, 1964, we worked continually in and around the area of Meridian and other counties in the eastern half of the Fourth Congressional District. To my knowledge, the only times that Michael left the state in those six and a half months were for a four-day conference in New Orleans in February, a one-day trip the two of us took to New York in March, and the Oxford orientation session in Oxford, Ohio, immediately prior to his disappearance. The only additional time that I was out of the state was for a ten-day visit to New York City from May 24 to June 2.

Shortly after we arrived in Meridian in January, we met Mr. James E. Chaney, a 21-year-old Negro man who worked with us and eventually became part of the Congress of Racial Equality staff. From about the middle of February to the end of March, James was out of Meridian, working first in Canton and then, for a short time, in Greenwood. At the end of March, he returned to Meridian to work with us.

In the first few weeks that Michael and I were in Meridian, we had to change our place of residence some three or four times, because the Negro families who took us in received intimidating phone calls and became afraid to house us. In February we were able to rent a house from a Negro, Mr. Albert Jones, which he rented from a white woman, Mrs. Roy Cunningham. We lived in that house until the beginning of June, when Mrs. Cunningham insisted that we leave. Prior to our eviction, we had had our rent raised by her.

In the first few weeks that we were in Meridian, we received no threats, nor did we suffer harassment at the hands of the local authorities. However, as people came to know us better, to recognize us, and to know what we were attempting to do, the tension increased. On several occasions my husband was picked up by the local police and taken to the police station, where he was questioned as to our activities, asked to show proof of ownership of our car, etc. They never did pick me up for questioning.

As we achieved some success in establishing the community center, the threats and intimidation began to increase. By May we received so many phone calls at late hours of the night that in order to get some sleep we were forced to remove our telephone receiver before going to bed. We finally resolved this problem by obtaining an unpublished telephone number when we moved to our new apartment after being evicted. The phone calls at the office during the day and evenings continued. They were of several forms. Some were extremely unpleasant in that when I picked up the phone the party at the other end of the line would use extremely offensive language towards me. Other calls we received were threats of violence, such as someone calling and telling me that he was planning to kill my husband, or that my husband was already dead. Michael received anonymous calls telling him that they intended to kill me or that I was already dead.

A man by the name of Mr. _____, who runs an _____ shop a few doors down the block from our office, used abusive language directed towards me and my husband continually. He constantly referred to my husband as "Jew-boy" and "nigger-lover." I have been told by workers in Meridian that on at least one occasion in the last month, several of them were threatened by Mr. _____ with an axe handle.

As the car which we drove became well known, we were followed by the police and by white citizens on many occasions. We became extremely cautious about driving at night, and would not do so unless it was a necessity. The white cab drivers took to following us, and did so even when I returned for the hearing on July 23.

At the end of April, my husband was arrested on two counts of blocking a crosswalk. He was held in the Meridian City Jail from Monday until after his trial on Wednesday. When he was released he told me that he had narrowly escaped a beating. The police officer who took him to his cell on Monday afternoon called one of the other prisoners out of the cell. My husband could not hear what the police officer said to the other prisoner, but when that man returned to the cell he took Michael aside and told him that he didn't know who he, my husband, was, or what he did, but that he better keep quiet about it while in the jail, because the police officer had said that if this prisoner got the others to beat Michael, no action would be taken by the police.

On Friday, April 18, my husband and I were visiting Reverend R. S. Porter, when he received word that a cross was burning in front of his church. We arrived at the First Union Baptist Church as the fire department was extinguishing the flames, but the cross was still smoldering.

In the beginning of June, a large group of people were arrested in Meridian when they attempted to form a picket line in front of three of the five-and-ten-cent stores. They were charged with obstructing traffic. My husband went down to the police station to find out the charges on the arrested persons. Officer A_____, who I believe was the desk sergeant that day, threatened my husband. From what Michael told me, his words were something like this: "If you get any more of these damn kids arrested, Schwerner, I'm going to get you, and that's a promise."

Working so closely with my husband and James Chaney, I was able, over the course of the months, to observe their habits and attitudes as workers. I have had the opportunity to observe other civil rights workers at their job, but I do not believe that there are any other workers in the state any more cautious or meticulous in their work than were Michael and James. Michael's concern about the danger to other people and the importance of minimizing it came from his experience as a rights worker and his feeling of responsibility as the Project Director. James undoubtedly derived much of his feeling of caution from the experiences he underwent in the 21 years of his life as a Mississippi Negro, subject to all the whims and capricious acts of the white citizens of this state.

Michael started making trips into Neshoba County in February and, in all, made about 30 such expeditions. Every time he went into that county to work, I remained in the office in Meridian to receive his phone calls when he checked in, or in the event that anything went wrong and he needed to contact someone. The only times that I did not serve in that capacity were the few trips he made into Neshoba County when I was out of the state. Because the county was known to be so dangerous, I insisted on assuming that job myself, out of obvious concern for my husband's safety. When James Chaney returned to Meridian at the end of March, the two of them usually traveled to Neshoba together, although there were one or two occasions when one of them went alone or with another person. Neshoba County has had a reputation for being so volatile that it has been nicknamed "Bloody Neshoba," and many experienced civil rights workers, for very good reason, declined to work in that territory.

My husband believed very strongly in security precautions, such as phoning in one's whereabouts, and on several occasions I heard him reprimand others who did not call in to the office when they were supposed to. I remember only one incident prior to his disappearance when Michael was two hours late returning from Neshoba County and did not call to tell me why. I was frantic and at the point of calling the jails, but refrained because I knew that if he had not been picked up, this would inform the authorities of his whereabouts and make the situation far graver. When he and James returned that particular evening, they said that they had been detained in talking with a contact who had no telephone, and that they were fearful of stopping on the road to call in and advise me of their delay.

On one occasion, I believe at the beginning of May, the two men, James and Michael, were planning to drive to Philadelphia during the day to see some people. As I had met several of the Neshoba County contacts in Meridian, and I had information to relate to them about community center programs which I believed would benefit them, I requested permission of the two men to accompany them. At first they both refused, but when I persisted, Michael finally agreed, and I believe that he agreed because he felt he might have been overprotective of me as his wife. James, however, did not have any of these personal involvements, so that he was able to rationally say that if I went, he would not, as he said that if he was seen in Neshoba County with a white woman we would all be killed. His sound advice was heeded and I did not enter Neshoba County on that day, or at any other time until after the disappearance of my husband, James Chaney, and Andrew Goodman.

On one or more occasions, James told me that the car had been followed in Neshoba County by white persons in cars with the license plates either covered or removed. On one occasion he said he had been followed by an official car, either that of police or sheriff's department, but I don't know which.

On June 21, 1964, Michael and James made another trip to Philadelphia, this time accompanied by Andrew Goodman, one of the volunteer COFO summer workers. I was in Oxford, Ohio, at the time, but before my husband left Oxford at 3 A.M., Saturday, June 20, he told me of his intention to go on Sunday to Philadelphia to investigate the burning of the Mt. Zion Church in the Longdale community. The three men never returned to Meridian, nor did they call in their whereabouts. All knowledge I have of my husband's habits and training indicates that, given the opportunity, he certainly would have called in. It is foolish to assert that he would have turned down the opportunity to do so. The information from officials is vague and contradictory, and all knowledge of the situation in Neshoba County would lead me to believe that the three men have been murdered.

On June 25, at about 3 P.M., I went to the State Capitol building in Jackson with John Robert Zellner, a Student Nonviolent Coordinating Committee field secretary, and Reverend Edwin King, the Tougaloo College chaplain. I attempted to see Governor Johnson to ask for his promise of help in the search for the three men. We were told by Senator Barbour that the governor was out for the afternoon and could not be contacted. He was extremely rude in his treatment of me. We then walked over to the Governor's Mansion, arriving just as Governor Johnson walked up the steps with Governor Wallace of Alabama. We followed them up the steps and Mr. Zellner introduced himself by name to Governor Johnson and they shook hands. Mr. Zellner then turned towards me and introduced me as the wife of Michael Schwerner, one of the three missing men. He said that I would like to speak for a moment with the Mississippi governor. The moment Johnson heard who I was, he turned and bolted for the door of the Mansion. The door was locked behind him and a group of Mississippi highway patrolmen surrounded the three of us. An officer with the name plate "Harper" refused to allow us to request an appointment with the governor. Harper said that he would not convey our request to Johnson.

On June 26, 1964, when I went to Neshoba County to speak with Sheriff Rainey, the car which I was in was followed by a blue, late-model pick-up truck without license plates. There were two white men in the truck. At one point the truck blocked us off in front and a white, late-model car blocked us from behind. We turned our automobile around and were able to get by the white car; the pick-up truck followed us awhile farther. We reported this to the FBI agents who were working in Philadelphia on the investigation. After I spoke with Sheriff Rainey, who denied knowledge of the circumstances of the disappearance of the three men, we obtained permission from Rainey and the FBI to follow the sheriff's car to the garage where the station wagon (which the men had driven on June 21) was being kept, in order that I could see it. Several young white men, who I believe were workers at the garage, laughed and made screams which are usually referred to as rebel yells when they realized who I was. When we left the garage the sheriff's car was close behind ours, and the blue pick-up truck once more followed after us to the outskirts of town, with the sheriff making no attempt to stop it or question the occupants about the lack of license plates.

SIGNED: *Rita L. Schwerner*

NESHOBA COUNTY

I am a third-year student at Georgetown University Law Center in Washington, D.C. I am in Mississippi assigned to the National Lawyers Guild as part of their summer program to render legal assistance to the Council of Federated Organizations.

From June 29 to July 25 at the request of the Council of Federated Organizations I participated in an extensive investigation of the destruction of the Mt. Zion Methodist Church in Philadelphia, Mississippi, and the disappearance of three civil rights workers in that same community. The results of that investigation are as follows:

Michael Schwerner and James Chaney were frequent visitors to Philadelphia, Mississippi, in the months just preceding their disappearance. Their visits were common knowledge in the white as well as the Negro community. On some of their trips to that area Schwerner and Chaney had been pursued through the rural areas of Philadelphia by Officer A_____ of Neshoba County. On Memorial Day, Michael Schwerner had spoken at the Sunday service at the Mt. Zion Methodist Church in connection with the Council summer program of Freedom Schools and voter registration. From that Sunday until Tuesday, June 16, Officer A_____ was frequently observed driving through the Mt. Zion area between Mississippi Route 16 and the Sandtown Road. Such excursions into the countryside were most unusual for Officer A_____.

At Mt. Zion, Tuesday nights were traditionally set aside for the leaders and stewards meeting. On those nights church business was disposed of and the collection for the pastor was taken. It was also on Tuesday nights that two of the missing men had been holding workshops in the Negro community in Philadelphia. The workshops were always held in a private home rather than at the Mt. Zion Church.

Tuesday, June 16, 1964, was the day the Democratic Party of Mississippi set aside for its precinct meetings to select delegates to the county conventions. As part of its political education program the Council of Federated Organizations had urged that registered Negro voters attend their precinct meeting and take an active role in the election of delegates to the county convention. Certain Neshoba County residents had intended to attend their meeting, but word reached them that Officer A_____ would be there waiting for them. Because of that tip and because of Officer A_____'s reputation it was decided that no one would attend the meeting.

Later that same evening the regular leaders and stewards meeting began as scheduled. There were approximately ten people in attendance. They had come in four vehicles, two cars and two trucks. The business was concluded about 10 P.M. and those in attendance began to leave the church. As they emerged from the church they noticed three strange vehicles in the church parking lot. In addition to that, 25 to 30 men, all armed, had formed a single line between the road and the church. These men watched the people leaving the church with great interest as though they were looking for someone. One man remained in a cream-colored 1964 Ford in the parking lot. He was described as a very large man wearing a broad-brimmed hat, kind of a cowboy hat, which was turned up at the sides. That man and that hat reminded several people of Officer A_____, and while they stopped short of a positive identification, it is clear that they knew who the man was, but fear of reprisal stopped them from making a positive assertion.

The Mt. Zion members passed by these men and headed to their cars and trucks to return home. Mt. Zion is situated on the Longdale Road which lies between the Sandtown Road on the north and on the south Mississippi Route 16. Some people proceeded north on Longdale Road to get to their homes, while others turned to the south. As the south group, which was composed of four persons, two in a car and two in a truck, was proceeding home and while they were still a short distance from the church, they were forced to the side of the road by a pick-up truck. Five or six white men approached the Mt. Zion vehicles and ordered the occupants to turn off their lights. The people were then forcibly pulled out of their car and truck and questioned. The questions asked generally ran along the same lines: "What kind of meeting went on here?" "Where are the white men?" "We know they had meetings here. Have they been having them over at the old school?" With one exception all the people who went out the south route were beaten, either with fists or, as in one case, with a heavy blunt instrument. The most serious injury suffered was a broken jaw. After the beatings the people pulled themselves together and went home.

The north group was a little luckier. Their progress home was blocked by a cream-colored 1964 Ford which was drawn across the Longdale Road in such a way that prohibited traffic from passing it. The two vehicles in the north group stopped. The car and the pick-up truck were approached by white men and ordered to turn off their lights. As were the prior group these people were also questioned about white men at the church and the nature of the meeting held there that night. In addition they were asked questions about pamphlets, and their assailants indicated that they had copies of certain publications. After a short time the north group was permitted to continue home. None of these people were beaten.

People were unwilling to make positive identifications of their attackers, but the other details they did relate seem to indicate that they well might know. Two persons, for instance, remember quite well seeing a policeman's uniform. Others recall seeing a huge broad man in a wide-brimmed hat sitting alone in a car in the church parking lot. One man remembers being searched very methodically, as if the person knew well what he was doing. Still others remember that the uninvited guests came in at least three vehicles, those being a cream-colored 1964 Ford sedan, a 1962 black and white Buick sedan, and a green 1964 Chevrolet pick-up. Everyone recalls a gunshot, and all remember that none of the cars had license plates. Fear might well be keeping the Mt. Zion congregation from revealing the names of their attackers. This opinion seems justified in light of the fact that at least one of the victims of that night's raid was taken to town a few days after the incident by Officer B_____ and was detained there for a period of three hours. Another person was paid a visit by two men, one of whom identified himself as _____. He told that person that if anyone was telling lies about the church burning and beatings they would go to the state prison.

People in the Longdale area who were not at the church that Tuesday night reported an unusual amount of vehicular traffic on the usually quiet

Longdale Road. One person sighted five cars heading down the road towards the church at a little after 11 P.M. at a speed of 45 to 50 m.p.h.

One man who lives in that area noticed a glow in the area of the church between 12 P.M. and 1 A.M. He immediately left his house to see what was afire, but his search was blocked by a car at the north end of the Longdale Road, the description of which car he could not give. Another local resident was awakened by a car outside his house at approximately 2 A.M. As he looked to see what the car was doing he noticed a glow in the sky in the vicinity of the church. At the time he thought to himself that it was the church, or perhaps two nearby houses. Many local residents also pointed out that there was a heavy rainstorm the night of June 16.

At the church site itself all that is now to be seen are a few bricks and some twisted metal roofing lying where it fell. There is not one piece of timber left, charred or otherwise. All that remains is that metal and some ashes. The destruction was so complete that one wondered if this was the work of a wood fire alone. The surrounding trees for at least 100 yards in three directions were scorched. The church itself was located in a heavily wooded area and it seems a fire of the size of the one that engulfed Mt. Zion Church should have spread. But it did not, which gives rise to the impression that it was tended so that it would not.

A short distance from the church and just to the right of the Sandtown Road is a forest fire tower. That station is manned from the hours of 9 to 5. Fires which occur during periods when the tower is not manned are called in so that they can be recorded. The regular ranger in charge of the station was on vacation the night of June 16, and the log kept there discloses no fire in the area that night. He did say that if he had been the one in charge that night the church fire would have been recorded.

The above account is an accurate, complete, and true description of all the information obtained by me during the aforesaid investigation.

SIGNED: *Michael F. Starr*

COAHOMA COUNTY

I am 21 years old and reside in Los Angeles, California.

On June 22, 1964, at 11:15 A.M., a police car pulled up to the curb as I was walking down Paul Edwards St. near 5th St. [in Clarksdale]. I had just come out of a house after talking with a Negro woman about voter registration. The man driving the police car, Officer A_____, called me over to the car and asked me what I was doing. I told him, "I am helping to register voters," and he said, "Don't you know that the niggers don't want any help? Don't you know you're not wanted here? What are you son-of-a-bitch bastards doing here anyway?" I responded, "We're just trying to register voters." Officer A_____ said, "Get in the car." I asked, "What is the charge?" and "Are we under arrest?" but Officer A_____ didn't answer but said to the other white man in the front seat to give him his stick. Officer A_____ quickly got out of the car and started towards me with the billy club, so I quickly got into the back seat of the police car. There were two other white men in the car, neither of which were in uniform. While we were driving, destination unknown to me, I was constantly harassed and threatened with statements like: "Your mother's not fit to work in a nigger whorehouse." "Don't you know that the people don't want you down here? Don't you know that the white people are getting angry? Don't you know that you're going to get hurt?" After a few minutes, I asked Officer A_____ under what charge was I picked up. He said that some "niggers" had called him and told him that I was stirring up trouble and what's more, I was trespassing.

I was cursed at continually until we reached city jail. I was ushered into a room, had my picture and fingerprints taken. I was questioned for about an hour by police and by white citizens. The questions were hostile and I could hardly answer any of them. I asked if I could use the telephone. They said, "Later." Officer A_____ came in and asked me if I was ready for trial and I said that I didn't know and wanted to make a phone call. I was finally put into a jail cell. I asked the guard if I could make a phone call and he said that he didn't have any authority. After about ten minutes, I was taken out and handcuffed and put back in the car. Harassment continued: "I guess you know you'd better leave town now. You can leave town or take thirty days in jail." (The charge was changed to vagrancy since it was found that I had $2.75 and had no visible means of support, even though I told the police that I had $15 a week coming to me by check.)

When we arrived at the county jail, I again asked for a telephone but was again denied it. I was then taken and imprisoned for about four hours, unable to talk to anyone who might know how long I was to be in jail or when I would be able to use a telephone. At about 4:30 P.M. I was taken downstairs and talked to a police officer for about a half-hour. He told me that I was going to be released but that I was being investigated for Communist affiliations and that if they found any, I would be turned over to the FBI. He also said that if I had any "concern for my safety or health" I should "leave town and go back home." He said that "there are 100 deputized white citizens trained in the use of billy clubs and just waiting for the signal to split some heads open." He said that "the white folks are getting angry and things are coming to a head," and he said he was glad about it. "Some folks are going to get hurt, maybe some killed, but then things will settle down. The federal government was not going to tell these folks what to do and they are going to fight to keep their rights." I was released about 5 P.M.

SIGNED: *Lewis Sitzer*

HINDS COUNTY

On June 23, 1964, at about 10:30 P.M., I was sitting in a car outside the Henderson Cafe, 2000 Valley Street, Jackson, with Eddie Young, Jr., of 1815 Cox Street, Jackson. Eddie was behind the wheel. A beige 1960 Pontiac with a gray hard top drove by with two white men inside. One of the men in the car fired one shot through the cafe window. There were four people in the cafe at the time. After the shot, the owner, Mrs. Alma Henderson, came out of the cafe and told us to chase the car and find out the tag number so that she could report it. We followed the other car, first on Valley, then onto Highway 80 going west, to Ellis Avenue, where it turned south. The car then turned west on Highway 18. About 2 ½ miles down Highway 18, it turned right down a road toward a TV tower. The car stopped immediately after making the turn, and waited until we went by. As we approached, we saw that there were no tags on the car. As we passed, at least three shots were fired from the car. Two of the shots struck me in the head; a third struck our car on the right-hand side below and behind the door.

We circled around and went back to Henderson's Cafe. When we got back to the cafe, the police were arriving also. We told the police what had happened. The name of one of the policemen was Joe Louis Land. Eddie Young, my wife Nancy, and Mary, a waitress at the Henderson Cafe, then drove me to the University Hospital.

I was in the hospital overnight, during which time my head was x-rayed and I was given intravenous doses of dextrose. I was examined by Doctor Corley and Doctor Webster. According to Doctor Webster, one bullet remains in my head, between my skull and the outer skin. He then said I was all right, and told me to go home whenever I wanted to. He said as long as the bullet had not creased my skull there was no danger. He said nothing about me returning to the hospital for further treatment. Dr. Webster is a white doctor. I returned home this morning and have not yet been contacted by any authorities.

SIGNED: _____*

*The publishers have been unable to locate the writer of this affidavit to secure his permission for its publication.

MADISON COUNTY

I was arrested in Canton, Mississippi, on May 29, 1964, charged with "parading without a permit" during a voter registration demonstration at which I was present but in which I was not participating. I spent 28 days in the Madison County Jail without being tried and during that period received no mistreatment from either officials or the white prisoners with whom I was housed. On Friday, June 26, eight of the fifty-five persons arrested on May 29th were still in jail in Madison County Jail.

At about noon on the 26th three men whom I believe are U.S. marshals, though I saw no credentials, took the eight of us to Jackson, Mississippi. I believe two of the marshals were Charlie Sutherland and Dan Kelly, and the third, a Negro whose name I don't know, I believe is the recently appointed marshal for the southern district of Mississippi. We were chained together in groups of two and three with chains and in that fashion we were driven in three cars to Jackson. In Jackson we were taken to the fifth floor of the Hinds County Court Building, where we were "booked" as federal prisoners. After a wait of about half an hour in the hall on the fifth floor we were taken to a second-floor county court room, where a U.S. Commissioner, who I believe is John R. Countiss III, interviewed each of us briefly for the purpose of reviewing and resetting bail. After that we were taken to our cells on the fifth floor. I, being white, was of course put into an all-white cell of the Hinds County Jail while the other seven prisoners, all Negroes, were put into an all-Negro cell. I had no difficulties on Friday, June the 26th.

On Saturday morning, the 27th, however, I was beaten three times by white prisoners. One or two hours after the 5 A.M. breakfast that morning a white prisoner who had been brought in during the night for, I believe, being drunk, started questioning me in an accusing, aggressive, and profane way as to whether I was a "Freedom Rider." He stopped after about five minutes, only to return in about 15 minutes. None of the other approximately 20 prisoners in the cell had questioned me in this regard the previous day, and I do not know why this particular prisoner decided to all of a sudden. Certainly jail officials were around the cell doors enough early that morning to have instigated such questioning, even though I have no specific evidence that they did so. After the second period of "questioning" the man returned in about 15—30 minutes and presented me with a civil rights leaflet which had been taken from the pocket of my coat which was hanging in the night section of the cell block. After he asked me a few questions about the leaflet someone started hitting me in the back of the head and in the face with their fists. The man who had presented the leaflet had been standing behind me and to the right as I sat at one of the long tables in the "day room" cell. While talking with him the third time I had not turned around to face him and so I cannot be sure whether he was alone and cannot be sure whether he was the one who hit me. He hit me about 15 times, stopped, and walked away. I remained seated at the table and did not respond to his implorations to stand up and fight him. As far as I was aware the other prisoners took no interest in the beating other than to watch. To the best of my recollection this took place at about 7:30 A.M.

About 15 minutes later a man who I believe was a deputy sheriff (he was wearing a uniform and a badge) called me to the door to ask what had happened. I told what had happened. He called out to the other prisoners to ask what had happened and the explanation he got from several of the prisoners was that I had been asleep on the table and had fallen off. I continued to explain what had happened because he did not seem to understand. When I mentioned that I was a civil rights prisoner he said "Oh" and promptly walked out. After about 15 more minutes the marshals who I believe are Kelly and Sutherland called me to the door and asked what had happened; Sutherland did all the talking. I told them; when they asked the prisoners what had happened, they got the same answer that the deputy had. Before leaving Sutherland did shout to the prisoners something like, "Leave that boy alone now." I didn't see any more deputies or marshals until I was bailed out.

At approximately 9:00 A.M. the first beating was repeated. This time a man approached me from behind where I was seated in the same place but did not say anything before he started to hit me. The beating lasted about as long as before, and both I and the other prisoners, as far as I know, had the same reactions as before.

After another 30–45 minutes a man approached me as the previous two had. I was still sitting at the table, but this time I had my head down on my arms on the table. This man pulled my head up by the hair and hit me once, from behind, directly in the right eye. As he walked away I could hear him mutter something angrily but couldn't really understand what it was.

Two drunks had been brought in early Saturday morning, around breakfast time. One of them slept most of the time but the other engaged himself in a lot of loud talking and antics of one sort and another. About 30–45 minutes after I was last hit the "active" drunk picked up a 4–5 foot length of broom or mop handle, which I noticed had been lying around the cell on the previous day. He charged at me from the front, but with the table and bench between us. He hit me about 6 times with the wood handle, the blows falling on my arms and shoulders as I was protecting my head.

I was standing in line for lunch when a deputy called my name and told me to get my things, that I was being bailed out. As the eight of us went one by one to the counter to sign for the return of our belongings, a deputy stepped on our toes as we signed the receipt form. I know this happened to me and I understand from the others that he did the same with them, too. Before we were taken down to the first floor the deputy called someone on the phone whom he called the "chief" to come up. When the chief came he asked me in a disinterested way about my beating. I told him briefly what had happened but did not go into any more details than he asked for.

On the first floor all eight of us signed a paper that Mr. Countiss presented us (in the presence of our attorneys, Carsie Hall and Marian Wright). Countiss had a county deputy photograph me; then we were released, about 12:30 P.M. Later that afternoon I talked with FBI Agent Kokes in his office and he took a report of the incident and also took photographs. My injuries, which did not cause serious bodily harm, consisted of bruises on the face and head, a black right eye, and one or two chipped teeth on the upper right side. On Monday, June 29, I gave a signed statement about the incident to Agent Regis Kennedy in the New Orleans, Louisiana, FBI office.

SIGNED: *Edward S. Hollander*

JONES COUNTY

At approximately 8:20 P.M. on the night of July 4, 1964, in the city of Laurel, Mississippi, Terry Gillum, Joe Lee Jones, Robert Earl Brown, and myself were going on foot to the Burgerchef Drive-in in order to be served under the provisions of Title II of the new Civil Rights Bill. As we approached the restaurant I saw a crowd of about 300 people, some in cars and others on foot. Before we got to the restaurant, we were set upon by a group of 25 white men, mostly teenagers and middle-aged men. I was hit in the back of the head with an iron pipe. Robert Earl Brown was hit in the eye with the pipe. Terry Gillum and Joe Lee Jones were beaten with fists. My injury required stitches, and Robert has not yet regained full vision in his injured eye. To the best of my knowledge, there were no police present and no arrests were made.

SIGNED: *Willie Roy Gillum*

HINDS COUNTY

On Monday, July 6, 1964, at about 8:30 P.M., the following happened:

About four of us were walking along Gallatin St. at the corner of Capitol St. [in Jackson]. Those with me were Robert Funch, Ben Foster, J. C. Foster, and James Lampley. When we got to the corner I saw a Negro boy being beaten by a white man in a cafe which was across the street from us. A Negro boy who had been with the boy who was being beaten told us that the white man had beaten the boy in the cafe which was a white cafe. The white man, when he saw a crowd of Negroes outside ran out of the cafe. He ran to his car which was parked on Gallatin St. and got something out of it which looked like a gun or a pipe. A crowd of Negroes followed the man to his car, but when they saw the object he got out of it they began to run away. Somebody called "Police" and we ran away down the R. R. tracks (as the tracks passed Pascagoula and Pearl St.). The white man who had done the beating was rather large and had on blue jeans and a straw cowboy hat.

We got off the tracks and on the way towards the COFO office the police cut us off at I think S. West St. as it crosses Gallatin St. There was a paddy wagon and a police car; altogether there were about 6 policemen. One of them said, "Hold it, nigger, don't run or I'll shoot." We stopped. All the policemen got out of their vehicles and some of them opened the back of the truck and threw J. C. Foster, James Lampley, and myself roughly into the truck. The rest of our friends had run away. The door of the truck was open, the police stood outside and called to J. C., saying that if he didn't come out of there they would come and get him. He went and the policeman hit him three times over the head with a blackjack. They closed the door of the truck and drove us down to Capitol Street until we were in front of the cafe where we had just witnessed the above incident. The police then opened the door to the truck and asked us if we were the boys who had jumped on a white man. We told him no. They said they were going to take us to jail and give us a lie detector test to see if we were telling the truth. They threatened to turn some white men from the cafe on us. A police captain told us to get out of the truck. One of the policemen asked me where I lived. I told him and he wrote it down. I was the only person who was asked his address. Then they told us to go home. (When they threw me in the paddy wagon I fell on my side, which was already hurt; because of this I didn't pay too much attention to what the policeman looked like.) I had never seen this police captain on Capitol St. before. I would be willing to be a witness if necessary.

SIGNED: *Ben Fleming*

COAHOMA COUNTY

I am a resident of Waterbury, Conn., and am 51 years old.

On Tuesday, July 7, 1964, at about 2:30 P.M. [in Coahoma County], I was driving Mrs. Aaron Henry and Miss Sheila Lindsey home in my car. A policeman, whom I later identified from FBI photos as Officer A_____, stopped me. He asked me, "Are you married to them niggers?" I said, "Those two Negroes with me are ladies." Then he said, "What are you doing here, anyway?" I said, "I am a minister for the National Council of Churches acting as counselor for the COFO group." He asked, "Do you preach?" I said, "No." Then he said, "You ain't no minister, you're a son-of-a-bitch of a troublemaker." I said, "Yes, I am a minister." He said, "You got nigger blood in you?" I said, "I don't have to answer that." He said, "No, you don't have to answer that or anything, but get out of town. Go back to Connecticut. They got crime there. Everything was orderly here until you people come." I asked, "Is that an order?" He said, "No, it is not an order, but it's a warning. I'm going to stay on your back until I get you." I said, "Now that you know who I am, I'd like to know who you are." He said, "You son-of-a-bitch, if I wanted you to know who I was, I would have told you." "Well," I said, "I'll pray for you." "You save your son-of-a-bitching prayers for yourself." Then he drove off.

Then I went to the FBI and told them about it. They took notes, but I didn't think to ask nor did they ask me to swear out an affidavit or sign a statement.

SIGNED: *Charles L. Pendleton*

FORREST COUNTY

I live in Chicago, Ill., and am a Negro participant in civil rights and desegregation work.

On Wednesday, July 1, 1964, at about 11 P.M., the following happened: myself, Marty Mullvain, Stuart Rawlings, Malcolm Zaretsky, Gregory Kaslo, and Nick Allis were driving home to Palmer's Crossing [Forrest County]. As we got to the less populated area I noticed the headlights of a car behind us. I was seated in the back seat with Stuart and Nick on the right-hand side of the car. I said, "I think we're being followed." Marty may have noticed the car before, but I do not recall his having said so. He (Marty) speeded up the car in an effort to determine whether or not the car was actually following us and the car speeded up behind us. At this point we were certain we were being followed. We kept driving until the car was right upon us and sounded its siren. There was no signal or flashing light. Marty stopped the car almost immediately. A man got out of the car and came up to the driver's side. In a very belligerent tone of voice he asked what we were doing out there. (He had not noticed me, the only Negro, in the car and this question was directed like, "What you fellows doing out here?") Marty handed him his license without comment and he shoved it back at Marty, saying, "Read the _____ thing to me."

He took no notice as Marty read but then started making a lot of profane comments. He said the guys were "lower than niggers" and ought to be beaten. He then flashed the flashlight in the back of the car and it was at this point that he saw me. He said, "Nigger, what are you doing in this car?" I did not reply. One of the guys (I don't know which) said, "We're taking the young lady home." He then said, "What's your home, nigger." At this point he left the driver's side of the car and came around on the other side. We rolled the window up and locked the door and he shouted, "Open that door or I'll drag . . ." The door was opened and he flashed the light in at me and said "What's your name, nigger." I replied, "Cress." He said, "Your full name."

I replied, "Lorne Cress." He then noticed that my knees were slightly showing and said something about my sitting in there "with your dress over your head." He then said, "I know you fellows been sitting here _____ this nigger's _____. I saw you. I could pull you in for contributing to . . ." (He did not finish.) "I could charge you with anything." He then said that I should "step out of the car and I'll take care of you."

I do not know at what point he slapped Malcolm; however, it must have been after he slammed the door after making this last statement to me. He then said, "I hope niggers are raping your mothers." This statement was repeated several times. He then reached in the opened window and slapped Malcolm. He then asked Malcolm if he was a minister. Malcolm said, "No." He then said: "Why, you hook-nosed bastard. I hope your mother is being raped by niggers."

He then said, "You get out of here," and, "I'm going to follow you."

Marty started up the car and we proceeded at a moderate speed. I suggested that instead of going to my house we go to the home of Mrs. Victoria Gray, where two of the boys were living. I felt that it would be better to go there than to where I live since Mrs. Gray's husband would be there and I live with a widow. He followed us all the way to the driveway but stopped there as we turned in and drove around the side of the house to the back yard. The man wore what seemed to be a beige shirt. He had a patch on his left sleeve saying "Forrest County Police." He wore a Stetson-like hat and seemed to be between 5'11" and 6 feet tall. He was over 40, perhaps between 50 and 55 years old, and wore glasses. He had relatively heavy jowls, but was not fat.

I have made several omissions that I now recall, such as his threatening that we had better not answer him and that he had a car full of men that would beat us if we didn't open the door (when he came around to the side that I was seated on). As he stood on this side of the car I also saw a tallywack (heavy, lead-loaded, leather-coated weapon).

SIGNED: *Lorne Cress*

PIKE COUNTY

On July 8, 1964, at about 3:40 A.M., I was asleep in a bed that was about 2 ½ feet away from the window. A bomb was placed about 1 ½ feet from the outside of the window.

I don't recall hearing any noise. I only remember lying on the floor beside my bed under glass from the window and the lumber from the window frame.

I assume that I had been unconscious for some time, for everyone had already made it to safety by the time I realized what had happened.

When I finally made it to safety (the kitchen) I was still quite dazed and noticed that I was bleeding profusely. I later learned that my body was covered with small cuts, and some 30 of them were deep cuts.

I believe the house (702 Wall St., McComb, Mississippi) was bombed because it was occupied by myself and other COFO workers and was being used as a Freedom House. My home is in Summit, Mississippi. I am a citizen of the United States of America.

SIGNED: *Curtis Hayes*

WARREN COUNTY

In my capacity as research man for the Vicksburg COFO Project, I have talked with several (5) leaders of the Bovina community whose names, for their protection, will not be used here. I talked with them about the burning of the Bovina community center on Tuesday night, July 7, 1964, between 10:30

and 11:30. The building was completely destroyed; no one was in the building at the time; no one was injured.

A small group of people gathered around the burning building between 10:45 and 11:45 P.M. on Tuesday night. Many were Negro leaders of the Bovina community; some were whites from Bovina; others were police officers, including Warren County Sheriff Vernon O. Luckett. At least three Negroes present—two of whom I spoke to—saw firemen pull a torch out from under the front part of the building. The torch, still blazing when the firemen pulled it out, was a 3-foot-long pole with rags wrapped around the end and wire wrapped around the rags, according to an eyewitness. Also according to eyewitnesses policemen took several pictures of the burning building and the torch. One man who saw the torch on Tuesday night said it was not there when he stopped by on his way to work the next morning at 5 A.M. Another woman who also saw the torch said she did not see it when she returned to the burned building late Wednesday morning.

Wednesday's Vicksburg *Evening Post* carried a short article on the burning. There were no direct quotes but one paragraph read: "Sheriff Vernon O. Luckett said the preliminary investigation showed no indications that arson might be involved." The article went on to say that since there was "a mild wind" and since the "fire did start in the rear of the building," it was likely that burning rubbish in a trash can 8 feet behind the building started the fire, according to Sheriff Luckett.

This is in complete contradiction to what the sheriff later told one man whose name will not be used here. He said that he did *not* believe the fire was set by the burning rubbish, and "no doubt it was set" by someone deliberately.

It is also in contradiction to my personal examination of the ruins of the building. The floor beams at the front of the building were completely destroyed, while several charred ones remained at the rear; one beam directly opposite the trash can from which the fire supposedly was started, even had a completely uncharred portion of wood on it. The trash can itself was about ¾ full of rusted and somewhat charred cans; one can still had paper on it, and there was more unburnt paper only slightly below the surface trash which had been burnt. The trash barrel did not have holes in the bottom to allow a draft to build up a large fire. So it seems extremely unlikely that a fire in the trash can could have been or was large enough to set a whole building on fire, especially a building more completely destroyed in the front and one covered on the outside with uninflammable asphalt shingles. I have photographs of all of this evidence at the ruins of the building.

The sheriff's account of the fire in the newspaper article of July 8 is further contradicted by the fact that no one from the Bovina community center had been burning trash in the barrel either on Tuesday, July 7, the day of the fire, or for several weeks before the fire. The last time trash had been burnt in the barrel was in the beginning of June according to officials of the Bovina community center. Again, according to officials of the center, the last time a party had been held in the center was in the third week in June. On Monday night, July 6, a routine meeting was held at the center, but only Cokes and cookies were served, so there was no trash that needed to be burned after the meeting.

What has Sheriff Luckett done to investigate the information recorded here? He had photographs taken of the torch, but there was no mention of either the torch or the photographs in the newspaper article. No official of the Bovina center has seen the photographs. Sheriff Luckett never contacted the president of the Bovina center; he did not speak with her the night of the fire although she was there at the burning; he has not spoken with her or contacted her in any way in the three weeks that have passed since the burning. Nor has any of his deputies contacted her. Two deputies did visit Bovina about two weeks after the fire and talked with some officials of the center, but that is apparently the only effort county officials have made to find out who burned down the Bovina community center.

SIGNED: *David Riley*

COAHOMA COUNTY

I am 58 years old, a Negro, and resident of Clarksdale, Mississippi.

At about 3 P.M. on Wednesday, July 8, 1964, I parked my car on Tallahatchie Ave. to get something to eat. While I was gone, a Negro parked a dump truck and then backed out, rubbing a white woman's car. The police came along and said that I had done it. I told them I didn't do it. "I swear I didn't do it." They said, "Stop swearing, you done it all right." Then they took me to city hall and locked me up. A small, light-haired policeman, whose name I don't know but who I would recognize from a picture, hit me on the side of my head and on my jaw with his fist, then took me by my thumb and butted my head up against the wall. He hit me with his fists several times, for no reason at all. When the white-woman clerk in the office started asking me questions and I was answering them, this man told me, "Don't look a white lady in the face, you god-damn son-of-a-bitch." Officer A_____ was present while I was being beaten, but didn't say anything about it.

I was not allowed to make a phone call until 8 A.M. the next morning. My rent man made $102 bond and I got out of jail about 2 Thursday afternoon.

SIGNED: *Joe Johnson*

FORREST COUNTY

At 11:30 A.M. on July 10, 1964, in Hattiesburg, Mississippi, I, Dave Owen, Rabbi Lelyveld, Janet Crosby, and another girl were returning to Morning Star Baptist Church after a morning of voter registration work. We were walking along a railroad track between River and Southern Avenues. Two men, on a road paralleling the railroad tracks, stopped their unmarked GMC pickup truck and assaulted us with an iron bar and a grease gun. The younger man hit me twice with the iron bar, pushed me down an embankment, and continued to kick me and beat me with his fists. The older man beat the rabbi and Dave about their heads. We reacted nonviolently. When they had finished, they returned to the truck and followed us to the intersection of the tracks and Southern Avenue. They attempted to hit us with the truck, but we stepped so that a ditch separated us. The older man jumped from the truck and aimed a blow at the rabbi, which I blocked with my arm. We continued to the church, from where we were taken to the hospital for medical treatment.

SIGNED: *Lawrence Spears*

JONES COUNTY

At approximately 2 P.M. on July 11, 1964, in Laurel, Mississippi, I saw a group of six Negro children, including my son, Larry McGill, Calvin Hughs, Jessie Arrington, and three others who I am not acquainted with, enter the H. S. Kress store on Central Avenue. They took seats at the counter and waited to be served. One of the waitresses placed a large knife in open view behind the counter. A man in a yellow shirt went up to and spoke to the policeman who was in the store at the time. The policeman, who was wearing a white shirt, spoke the word "Now," and at this time the man in the yellow shirt and another man in a checkered shirt pulled baseball bats from paper sacks and began to beat the children. Larry was hit across the back with a bat. Jessie was hit in the face with the bat and his hand was cut badly. The children fled the store and I drove the injured boys to the hospital, where Jessie required stitches in his hand. The policeman did not make an immediate attempt to stop the beating and took action after the children fled the store.

SIGNED: *Bertie McGill*

COAHOMA COUNTY

I am 24 years old, and I reside in Clarksdale, Mississippi.

At about 1 P.M. on Sunday, July 12, 1964, I was in the laundromat on State St. next to the _____ Store. Although the store has no signs up, this is understood to be a "white" laundromat. My clothes were in the washer when the owner of the store came in accompanied by two policemen. He told me to get out and be quick about it, so I left. The police car followed me and about three blocks away pulled me over to the side. They asked to see my driver's license. They said I had failed to signal a turn. Then they took me down to the jail. There Police Officer A_____ and two other officers began to beat me. They hit me with both their fists and with a billy club, causing my mouth to bleed. Officer A_____ asked me what business I had in that place (the laundromat). He also said, "Do you know you're a nigger and are going to stay a nigger?" This was all going on while they were hitting me. Then they locked me up, and I was later released after making $64 bond on charges of "resisting arrest" and "failure to signal." At no time did I put up any resistance to arrest.

SIGNED: *James A. Campbell*

HINDS COUNTY

I reside in New York, New York, and am a volunteer voter registration worker with the Council of Federated Organizations.

On Wednesday, July 15, 1964, at about 10:30 P.M., Steve Smith, Melvin Mc-Davia, Robert Ellis, and myself were taking voter registration material in a pick-up truck to Greenville and Greenwood. We were traveling by way of Canton. Steve Smith was driving.

As we were entering Highway 51 (in Jackson) we were stopped by two Jackson city policemen. They asked Steve where we were going and he told them Canton. They also looked through the truck and saw the voter registration material we were carrying. They then gave Steve a ticket for driving without a commercial license.

After receiving the ticket, we proceeded on toward Canton. Along the way we were worried that the Jackson police might call ahead to the highway patrol to have us stopped. (We thought that the proper procedure for the Jackson police to have followed was to have made us leave the truck and not allow us to drive it until someone had the proper license.) We thought at several times along the way that suspicious cars were following us.

About five miles out of Canton (just past Madison) we saw one car that was definitely following us. The car was unmarked and there was no indication that it was a police car. We increased our speed to try and get away from the car. The other car also increased its speed but did not try to stop us. It just remained behind us, blinking its lights. As we reached Gluckstadt, the car pulled up close to us and began blinking a red light. We then pulled over. It was about 10:30 P.M. at this time. The doors and windows of our truck were locked.

A man, not in uniform and not wearing a badge, came out of the car and came over to the truck. He ordered Steve out of the truck. Steve asked him for identification and the man refused to show any. He pulled his gun and told Steve to get out. Steve got out and I got out also. The man asked Steve for identification, driver's license, etc. Steve showed him what he asked for. He asked Steve about what was in the truck, where we were going, where did we get our hats, etc. Steve answered all these questions very politely. He then started insulting us and asking us sarcastic questions which had nothing to do with any traffic violations.

A highway patrolman then pulled up in another car. The highway patrolman was in complete uniform and his badge number was _____.

He wore a name pin with the name Officer A_____ on it. A third car pulled up after Officer A_____'s car. This car was unmarked and a man wearing no uniform and without any sign of authority (except a gun sticking out of his back pocket) got out. Officer A_____ and this third man searched the truck and made everyone get out. Officer A_____ looked through the material in the back of the truck and threw Melvin, who was riding there, out, kicking him over the tail gate in the process. They made all four of us line up in a row, cursed us, threatened us, and the third man kept shouldering Steve and myself and stepping on our toes.

A fourth car pulled up about this time. It was also unmarked and one man in plain clothes, except for a gun in a holster, got out. The four men then huddled together and talked among themselves while writing a ticket. Then the first of the four cars (the one that originally stopped us) left. The third man then put Steve in the highway patrol car in the rear seat and got in with him. The fourth man told Melvin and Robert to "run back to Jackson." He also told them to quit working with COFO or COFO would get them killed. The two kids began running down the highway towards Jackson. The fourth man then started threatening me. While he was doing this I could hear the sounds of Steve being beaten in the other car. The man in the car with Steve then got out. When he opened the door of the car to get out, a light in the car went on. In that light I could see Steve slouched over with blood running from his head. The three men then told me that they had no charges against me and that I should take the truck and drive off. I told them that my driver's license had expired and that they should arrest me along with Steve. The fourth man then promised me that he would let me drive the truck without a license. I was afraid that they might come after me if I tried to leave, so I still refused. They emphasized that they had no charges against me but that if I tried to take their guns then they would have a charge.

When I asked to be arrested again, the man who had beaten Steve got angry and kicked me in the shins. The fourth man then punched me in the eye. He (the fourth man) then pulled out his gun and started hitting me with it on the right side of my head. I tried to protect myself from the blows, but at no time tried to resist or take his gun. Each time he hit me he said, "Stop trying to take my gun." I fell to the ground and he then kicked me in the arm and in the chest.

He told me to get up. As I was getting up he kicked me in my ribs. He (still the fourth man) then told me to get into the car that Steve was in and ordered Steve to get out. When Steve got out he was limping and had blood all over his shirt, face, arm, and head. I then got into the car and Steve was put into the fourth car. The highway patrolman (Officer A_____) and the fourth man then got into the front of the car that I was in and began driving toward Canton. The fourth man then told Officer A_____ that they should drive me to Philadelphia and made some reference to the three missing COFO workers. They continued to make comments about me and other COFO workers until we arrived at the Madison County Jail in Canton.

At the jail they locked me up until the next morning. The next morning, after four requests, I was allowed to make a phone call by the jailer's wife. (I had also asked to make a phone call the night before when I was first taken to the jail.) I called COFO in Jackson and spoke to Bob Moses. I told him what had happened the night before.

Shortly thereafter, I was taken to the home of a judge in Madison. Court was held in his garage and two lawyers from COFO were there. Highway patrolman Officer A_____, the man who had beaten Steve, and the man who had beaten me were the only other persons present. I heard the man who had beaten me referred to as Officer B_____ by Mr. Braiterman (a COFO lawyer). I was then charged with interfering with Steve's arrest and resisting arrest. Bail was set at $150 and the case was continued until the 27th of July.

We were then taken back to the Madison County Jail and were bailed out later that evening. At no time did I request or receive any medical attention.

I would be able to identify the highway patrolman, the man who beat Steve, and the man who beat me if I ever saw them again.

SIGNED: *Eric Morton*

LEFLORE COUNTY

On or about July 13, 1964, I had a conversation with Police Commissioner B.A. Hammond, of Greenwood City, Leflore County, in front of the Council of Federated Organizations project office at 708 Avenue N, Greenwood, Mississippi. During the conversation, which took place before a large number of Summer Project workers, the police commissioner made the following points:

1. He, B.A. Hammond, has been a member of the Citizens' Council since its formation in 1954.
2. There are between 600 and 700 members in the city of Greenwood and that between 75 and 100 usually attend the Citizens' Council meetings.
3. The voter qualification laws passed by the legislature and approved by the overwhelmingly white electorate in 1954 were designed to hinder Negro voter registration. I asked Commissioner Hammond, "Isn't it true that the laws passed in 1954 to raise voter qualifications were designed to hinder Negro registration?" Commissioner Hammond replied, "Yes."
4. I asked Commissioner Hammond, "Why had the laws passed in 1890, which had been sufficient until 1954, been changed in 1954?" Commissioner Hammond replied, "The Supreme Court decision woke people up." The commissioner was referring to the Supreme Court school decision, Brown v. Bd. of Education.
5. I asked Commissioner Hammond if he agreed with the Citizens' Council position on Negro voting. Commissioner Hammond replied, "I essentially agree."
6. I asked Commissioner Hammond, "Has a Negro ever served on a jury in Greenwood?" Commissioner Hammond replied, "Not to my knowledge." I asked Commissioner Hammond if he felt that Negroes' not serving on juries hindered the equal administration of justice in cases in which Negroes were defendants. Commissioner Hammond replied, "I don't see why. Juries are supposed to be impartial." The commissioner said that the important factor

was whether you were qualified and that he did not feel that he was personally qualified to serve on a jury and did not do so.

SIGNED: *Michael Sayer*

JONES COUNTY

In connection with my work for the COFO project in Laurel, Mississippi, I became aware of the following facts:

On the night of July 18, 1964, at approximately 9:30 P.M., a rock was thrown through a back window of the office of Dr. T. J. Barnes, M. D., at 426 Front Street, Laurel, Mississippi. Wrapped around the rock was a note, written on the back of a blank check, and the note had the following message: "If you don't want the same thing to happen to you that happened to the three civil rights workers in Neshoba County, then stop working with the NAACP." The note was signed "KKK." Although Dr. Barnes is not connected with the NAACP in any way, Dr. Murph, the dentist who has the upstairs office, is president of the local NAACP chapter and advisor to the NAACP youth council.

These facts were related to me by Dr. Murph, who could not be reached to make a deposition.

SIGNED: *Geoffrey R. W. Smith*

FORREST COUNTY

I reside in Ann Arbor, Michigan. I am 25 years old and am a naturalized American citizen. I am a graduate student in nuclear physics at the University of Michigan.

I have been teaching at the Freedom School located at the True Light Baptist Church in Hattiesburg, Mississippi. That school is operated under the program of the Council of Federated Organizations (COFO). I have been teaching there since the first week in July, 1964, and have been teaching science, math, and music to Negro children there.

On July 20, 1964, Susan B. Patterson, William D. Jones (two other teachers at that school), and I went shopping in Hattiesburg. Mr. Jones entered the Standard Walgreen drug store, and Susan and I were still outside. I went to the street curb to signal some people in a car who I thought were friends of mine. As I stood at the curb, I suddenly felt a barrage of heavy blows on the back of my head and neck and on my left ear. I was knocked across the sidewalk and fell to the pavement near the drug store window. I then covered my ears and head with my arms and curled up my legs as I lay there. I was then kicked in the face, the side of the head at the left temple, and in the area of the kidneys. At no time during this beating did I see the person who was beating me. I said nothing while I was being beaten. I never lost consciousness during the beating, and I heard Susan cry for the police. The beating lasted for about one minute. When it stopped I arose and saw a policeman searching a man who I subsequently learned was Houston Hartfield. The policemen asked me if I would sign a complaint against Hartfield for assault and battery. I agreed to do so and walked to the police station with Susan and Mr. Jones for that purpose. I was not asked to make any such complaint when I arrived at the station. I was then told that I was under arrest for assault and battery. I posted $25 cash bond and was released on bond.

The police told me that I was under arrest because they could not ascertain who had started the fight. This was told to me by the officer who had searched Hartfield. I saw Hartfield arrested and booked. When I was being held in arrest, Hartfield told the police that I had elbowed him on the courthouse steps. That was not true at all, but I continued to say nothing to Hartfield. Mr. Jones called Hartfield a liar at that point and Hartfield tried to assault him. Hartfield had to be restrained by a number of officers.

Susan Patterson and I are white persons and Mr. Jones is a Negro.

SIGNED: *Peter C. Werner*

COAHOMA COUNTY

I am a white volunteer working in voter registration with the COFO Summer Project in Clarksdale, Mississippi, and am 20 years of age.

On Monday, July 22, 1964, at about 1 P.M., my wife Lisa and I were walking along Yazoo Ave. An unmarked police car, driven by Police Officer A_____, pulled up next to us. Officer A_____ called us over and started questioning us as to our names. We replied and he then said, "Didn't I tell you yesterday to get out of town?" He then asked us what we did for a living and by whom we were supported. Some discussion ensued as to what constituted support, after which Officer A_____ told us to get in the car. We were told that we were under arrest for vagrancy. On the way to the office, Officer A_____ kept up a constant stream of verbal abuse. He used such terms as "half-breed," "nigger-lover," "nigger whore," "nigger pimp." A white civilian, who was in the car when Officer A_____ drove up, also added to the stream of curses. Upon arrival at the station, Lisa and I were placed in the entry room and separated. We were instructed not to converse. We were not allowed to sit down. Officer A_____ left us with the white civilian who had been in the car as well as another unidentified civilian who was waiting at the jail. Both young men were in their middle twenties. They kept up a continuous stream of questions, insults, and veiled threats. After ten minutes, we were led into the investigation room by another officer who wore neither a badge number nor a name plate. He began questioning us, using a long investigation report containing questions on name, address, occupation, parents' occupation, etc. Lisa asked what the forms were, and he told her they were investigation forms. He asked me if we had actually been placed under arrest and we answered "Yes." He asked one of the aforementioned civilians to confirm this and he did. From then on, the officer left us under the impression that we were indeed under arrest. This officer then engaged us in conversation for a good hour on the racial situation in Mississippi. He was polite enough, though not friendly. He then fingerprinted us and took photographs. After about an hour and a half of questioning, unpleasant remarks, and stories about "niggers," Officer A_____ re-entered the room. He then proceeded to ask more questions, interspersing them with insults to my wife. The insults became the dominant part of the conversation, with Officer A_____ finally saying to me, "Why don't you get angry? Why don't you stand up like a man?" He was obviously trying to provoke me and would have, with the slightest provocation, proceeded to beat me. I refused to be baited and finally we were asked to leave the room. After a few minutes I was called back by myself. Officer A_____ started intensive questioning about where we stayed, how many stayed in the Freedom House, etc. I refused to answer the questions, whereupon he said, "Boy, if you give me any trouble, I'm going to kill you." He then continued the questioning and began to insult my wife again, asking, "How many niggers did you sell your wife to last night?" "How many niggers did your wife_____?" I again refused to rise to the bait, at which point he said, "Why don't you stand up like a man? I'd like to bounce you off the floor three times. I'd like to kill you." After a few more minutes of this, Officer A_____ left. We were told that we were merely being investigated and would now be released. We left the station after having been held three hours.

SIGNED: *Robert Mandel*

SUNFLOWER COUNTY

On Friday, July 24th, 1964, from about 2 to 3:15 P.M., the following happened:

Mr. Jeffrey Sachar and I were requested by certain people in the Drew community to attend a meeting to be held at 2 P.M. in Counsellor Townsend's office; which meeting was set up at 11 A.M. that morning. The people invited to the meeting were the parents of the Drew children arrested on July 15th for participating in civil rights activities. When Mr. Sachar and I arrived at the office, Mr. Townsend told Police Officer A_____, then present, to remove us from the office. Officer A_____ is [a public official] in Drew. I said that we just wanted to make sure these people had counsel; could we call a lawyer for these people. Mr. Sachar told them (the parents) not to say anything (meaning not to say anything without a lawyer). Officer A_____ forcibly removed us from the office, threatening us with arrest. We sought a pay phone and were told at Dot's Cafe that there was a pay phone at _____'s service station on the highway. Mr. Sachar drove to the _____'s station and put through a call to the Greenwood COFO office, where he informed them that parents were in the city counsellor's office without benefit of counsel. The gasoline attendant told us that if we were phoning about civil rights to get out of his station and call somewhere else. Mr. Sachar said he was not phoning about civil rights and then continued on speaking for a few minutes. The attendant went to a drawer and pulled out a revolver. I informed Mr. Sachar, "He's got a gun. Let's go." We were gone immediately just as another car with a rebel flag waving pulled into the station.

We waited some time until the meeting was over and searched and found Officer A_____, and Mr. Sachar and I said, "Can we talk to you?" He said, "I have nothing to talk to you about." Sachar said, "Some guy just pulled a gun on us and I want to file a complaint with you." He said, "Well, see the mayor." Sachar said, "Do you mean that you can do nothing about it?" He said, "That's right." I said, "But a man pulled a gun on us; we want to file a complaint." He said, "I'm not interested." He continued, "If you want to, you can file a complaint with the mayor, but I'm not interested."

We left, informed the Jackson SNCC office of the incident, and returned home.

SIGNED: *Rabbi Allan Levine*

SHARKEY COUNTY

I am a citizen of the United States of America and am a Negro.

Friday night, July 24, 1964, on the way from Bay St. Louis, the hub on the left rear wheel came off of my car. I left Issaquena at 9:15 P.M. and came to Greenville. I returned at 10:45 P.M. to fix my car. It was gone. I had left it off the road, at the bottom of a ditch. I looked for the car until about 1:30 A.M. but did not find it and came back home. I returned to Rolling Fork at 8 A.M. and a fella said to check with the highway patrol or the man at the _____ place [a garage]. I went there and the fella said he would call the highway patrol. The patrolman could not come because he was investigating an accident— a white boy had run over and killed a colored boy. I was told to meet the patrolman. I went out there around 9:45 A.M. and was standing around. The patrolman asked what I wanted and I said that I wanted to see him about my car when he got the time. I said that I had left it sitting but I was told he had picked it up. I asked why, when I had it off the road in a ditch. He said, "The best thing for you to do is go up there and pay _____ [the owner of the garage] for the damn car and get your black ass out of Sharkey County." I turned to get back in the car I was driving. He called me back and got a blackjack out of his car; he asked where I was going. I said that I was going to pay the man. He said, "No, you is a smart son-of-a-bitch. Come back here and let me see your driver's license. I'm gonna give you a ticket; if you'd went on and paid the man, I wouldn't give you one." The patrolman got in his car and told me to come on to the garage where the car was. We got to the garage and he asked me to come inside. We went into [the owner's] office, and [the owner] came in. He fastened the door. He asked me why I locked the car "in his territory." The car hadn't been locked; there is no key to it. "Don't tell me that car wasn't locked." He hit me three times on the head (once on the right side and twice on the left) with the blackjack. He said to turn the blackjack loose after I grabbed it. I told him that he could kill me before I'd turn it loose. I didn't want him to hit me no more. He said that I was "a smart son-of-a-bitch and go back to Greenville and tell all the niggers in Greenville that they beat a nigger's ass in Sharkey County." He said, "When you get there tell the police department which is y'all's good friends, that we whip niggers' ass in Sharkey County." He then said, "Get out of Sharkey County and don't be caught back here no more; stay in Washington County." When I got ready to leave he told me to take the ticket to Judge Spairs in Mayersville and it better be paid by 1:30 P.M.

I then left and came home.

The police officer was a highway patrolman named Officer A_____ from Unit _____.

I have a lawyer from Greenville who has agreed to take the case. His name is _____.

SIGNED: _____*

*The publishers have been unable to locate the writer of this affidavit to secure his permission for its publication.

PIKE COUNTY

I live in McComb, Mississippi, and I have permitted the members of COFO to use my grounds for youth meetings of local young people. The first such meeting was held on July 18, 1964.

On July 26, 1964, at 1 A.M., I was in bed when I heard a car stop in front of my house. I got up to see who it was and I saw a black car. It was an old-model car. The lights from a car coming from the opposite direction shone on the black car and the black car pulled off. I came out of the house and watched the car go over the hill. I came back into the house and all at once it came into my mind that they could have been the bombers who have been going around. So I got my gun and came into the living room to watch and see if they would return. A few minutes later they returned and parked in the same spot. This time I got up and aimed my gun at the car. The window was up and the screen was closed. I did this after the first time I saw them. I waited about three or four minutes to see what they were going to do. I then heard a noise like a bundle of sticks hitting the ground right in front of the window. It landed on the ground and then I opened fire and the car took off. It was going north. Just as the car took off a small blast went off in the yard. I then ran to get my husband who was sleeping and he grabbed the gun from me and ran out the back door and came around to the front yard. By the time he got to the front yard a car was coming back by the house at a very high speed. When it approached the house two shots were fired: one hit the window and the other hit high above the window on the outside. At the same time the last shot was fired the big blast went off and I saw my husband being knocked around and to the ground by the blast. He fired two shots in the ground because he had lost his balance due to the blast. After this we tried to get ourselves together because people began coming over and we were in our pajamas. About five minutes after the bombing a local cop whom we know as [a nickname] came up the walk to our house and told us to put our guns away.

The only reason that I can give for them bombing my house is that I have let the COFO civil rights workers use my yard and cafe for meetings and picnics.

SIGNED: *Ora Lee Bryant*

COAHOMA COUNTY

I am 22 years old, a Negro citizen of Mississippi, and a field secretary for the Student Nonviolent Coordinating Committee. This summer I am the director of the Council of Federated Organizations' project in Clarksdale, Miss. The first day that I arrived in Clarksdale to arrange for housing for the other workers Police Officer A_____ came up to me and said, "We ain't goin' to have this shit this year." He then asked me if I wanted to fight right then and I said that I was nonviolent. He continued to use obscene and abusive language. The next day he and other policemen sat in front of the office and took our pictures with a movie camera. I didn't say anything the first day but the second day I asked one of the policemen what they were doing. He replied that Officer A_____ had told them to do it. I then went to Officer A_____ himself. He said this was America and he could do whatever he wanted. I told him that we were going to call the FBI. He said he didn't care who we were going to call. Officer A_____ then said, "I'm going to kill you if it's the last thing I do." I didn't say anything and went off. This same day Officer A_____ assigned a policeman to follow me around wherever I went. When I would go into any place that policeman would stay outside. This same policeman would follow people from the project to try to find out what families we were living with and where we ate.

After the Civil Rights Bill was signed, Officer A_____ went around to all the Negro restaurants and told them that if they served the project workers, either white or Negro, he would close them up. He mentioned my name in particular and said he didn't care who they told.

A while later an agent from the city water and light department came to the office and tried to turn the lights off. He called Officer A_____, who came over and cursed at us. We talked to him outside the office. He told us to get inside and instructed another policeman to "Get the damned billy clubs, we're going to have to move these niggers." He grabbed the arm of a Negro volunteer named Doris Newman and twisted it. I called the FBI office. They asked for a statement. I said that the situation was too bad for us to go down and asked them to come over. But they wouldn't do this. The next day a Negro man came by the office. He refused to tell us his name and told me not to tell anyone of this conversation. He told me that Officer A_____ had hired some men to kill me. We haven't seen anything of him since. The next night, after I had been told of the threat to my life, I went to a drug store and the people in there told me that some white men had been asking about me. When I was on my way back to the Freedom House a group of white men stopped me and showed me a gun. They said, "This has two buckshots in it, and both of them have your name on them. I'm going to bowl this up your ass and blow it off." I walked off and called Officer A_____. He told me to go to hell and hung up.

About three days after the incident with the white men with the gun, I went up to the courthouse to help register some people and Police Officer B_____ and Officer A_____ were there waiting for me. Officer A_____ said, "There aren't too many white people in town who like you and I'm not one of them. If you don't want to come up like your nigger-loving friends in Philadelphia you'd better get back to the nigger section of town." I said, "What's that?" and two highway patrolmen came up and said, "Let us show him where it is." I was the only one standing outside so I decided to leave.

About a week ago the water and light man came back again. I was standing outside in front of the office. He was carrying a knife. Two police cars were parked across the street. He swore at me and threatened me. He went over to the policemen and talked to them for a while, then came back over to me and started the same thing over again. I went over to the policemen and told them that I wanted to have this man arrested. They said they hadn't seen him do anything.

On July 24 after midnight three white men threw bottles through the office windows. We called the police but they didn't come that night. They came the next day. While they were there the same three white men came in and a man who lived across the street identified them as the ones who had thrown the bottles. They arrested them on the spot and said they were fined $11 dollars, and let them go immediately.

SIGNED: *Lafayette Surney*

Index

Page numbers in **bold** refer to statements made by that individual.

Adams County, 45, 55
Allen, Anner, 36
Allen, Crawford, 36
Allen, Elizabeth, xvii, **36–44**
Allen, Lewis, xvii, 36–44
Allis, Nick, 90
Amite County, xiv, xvii, 3, 4, 36, 38, 41
Arrington, Jessie, 96
Arsenault, Raymond, xv
Atkins, James, **44–45**
Atkins, Percy Lee, **35–36**

Barnes, T. J., 102
Baskin, David, 46
Bevel, James, 26
Black, James Charles, **69–71**
Blackwell, Randolph, 9, 10
Blaelock, Melvin, 38, 40, 42
Block, Sam, xvi, 69, 70
Brewer, Charles, 46–47
Brewer, Greene, vii–x
Brewer, Percy Lee, vii, 10
Brooks, Odessa, **31–33**
Broom, Essie, 14, 15
Brown, Jess, 32, 55
Brown, Luvaugn, 11
Brown, R. Jess, 32
Brown, Robert Earl, 87
Bryant, C. C., xiv
Bryant, Ora Lee, xiv, **109–10**
Burt, Mr., 65–66
Butler, A. C., 51

Campbell, James A., **97**
Carnell, Willie, 30
Carter, Hodding, II, xx
Carter, Hodding, III, xx, xxi, xxii
Chaney, James E., xi, xviii, 72, 74, 75, 77
Citizens' Council, viii, ix, xi, xx, xliii, 66, 101. *See also* White Citizens' Council
Civil Rights Act, x, xix, xxii, xxxvi, 110
civil rights movement, viii, xvii, xx
Clarksdale, MS, xi, xii, xvi, xviii, xix, xxiii, 7, 8, 12, 13, 16, 19, 31, 33, 35, 44, 81, 95, 97, 104, 110
Cleveland, MS, xvi, 10, 14, 21
Coahoma County, xi, xvi, 7, 12, 16, 19, 34, 45, 89, 95
Cobb, Charles, 63–64
Communists, xxxv
Congress of Racial Equality (CORE), xiii, xv, xxi, xxxv, 4, 52, 58, 59, 71, 72
Cotton, Dorothy, 26
Cotton, Douglas MacArthur, **29–31**
Council of Federated Organizations (COFO), vii, viii, x–xiii, xv, xvii, xix–xxii, xxv, xxxiv, xxxv, xxxvi, xli, 8, 29, 52, 71, 75, 77, 78, 88, 89, 92, 99, 100, 102–4, 106, 109, 110
Countiss, John R., III, 84, 86
Cox, Harold, xi
Cress, Lorne, xvii, **90–91**
Crockett, George, 50
Crosby, Janet, 95

Delta, the, 37
Delta Democrat-Times, xxi
Delta Ministry, xii, xxxvi
Democratic National Convention, xii, xvii, xviii, xxi
Derby, Doris, 57
desegregation, xvi, xxxiii, 14, 90
Diggs, Charles, 8
Dittmer, John, xv
Doar, John, 11, 12
Dogan, Ellett R., vii
Doghan, Alex, 47

Ellis, Robert, 97, 99
Everett, George E., 12
Evers, Charles, 64
Evers, Medgar, xxxi

Federal Bureau of Investigation (FBI), x, 12, 14, 15, 18, 26, 38, 43, 44, 50, 58, 66, 68, 76, 82, 86, 89, 110, 111
Federal Bureau of Prisons (FBP), xxxiii
First Union Baptist Church, 73
Fleming, Ben, **87–88**
Forrest County, xiii, xvii, 49, 90, 91, 95, 103
Foster, Ben, 87
Foster, J. C., 87, 88
Freedom House, 60, 92, 105, 111
Freedom Riders, xv, 6, 84
Freedom School, xiii, 77, 103
Freedom Summer, vii, ix, x, xii–xiv, xvi, xviii, xix, xx, xxii, xxiii
Freeman, Rosemary, 20–22, 25, 27, 28
Funch, Robert, 87

Galloway, Willie, 48–49
Gillum, Terry, 87
Gillum, Willie Roy, **87**
Gilmore, Hattie Mae, xxi, **19–20**

Goldman, Andrew, xi, xviii, 75
Gordon, Joe, 37, 38
Graves, Dr., 51
Green, David, 17
Green, George, 30, 31
Greene, Charles, vii
Greene, George, **45–46**, 64
Greenville, MS, xix, xx, xxii, xxxiii, 9, 98, 107, 108
Greenwood, MS, xvi, 9, 10, 12, 14, 15, 20, 23, 27–29, 69, 72, 98, 101, 103, 106
Guy, Chief, 30, 65, 68
Guyot, Laurence, 11, 26

Hall, Carsie, 59, 86
Hallinan, Terrance, 33
Hamblin, McKinley, **60–61**
Hamer, Fannie Lou, xvii, xxiii, **20–21**, 22–23, 27, 28, 69
Hammond, B. A., 101–2
Harris, Arthur, **48–49**
Harris, Jesse, xv, **4–7**
Harris, Julius, 51
Hartfield, Houston, 103–4
Hattiesburg, MS, xiii, xviii, 49, 50, 95, 103
Hayes, Curtis, **92**
Henry, Aaron, xv, xxi, **8**, 45, 89
Hinds County, xv, 4, 17, 50, 52, 55, 57, 63, 82, 84, 87, 97
Hinds County Jail, xv, 50, 84
Hollander, Edward S., **84–86**
Hughs, Calvin, 96

Jackson, MS, xi, xiii, xvii, xxii, xxxvi, xliii, 4, 8, 9, 10, 17, 32, 34, 50, 52, 57, 59, 62–64, 66, 68, 75, 82, 84, 87, 98–100
Jackson County Jail, 53, 58
Javits, Jacob, 68

Jenkins, Ira, 3
Jewett, Richard A., **52–55**, **57–59**
Jim Crow, viii, xx, xxiii, xxiv
Johnson, Joe, xix, **95**
Johnson, June E., xvii, 20–23, 25, **27–29**
Johnson, Larry, 12–14
Johnson, Paul B., Jr., 76
Jonas, Rene, 65
Jones, Daniel, 43
Jones, James Wilson, **17–19**, 69
Jones, Joe Lee, 87
Jones, William D., 103, 104
Jones County, xix, 87, 96, 102

Kaslo, Gregory, 90
Kelly, Dan, 84, 85
Kennedy, Edward, 68
Kennedy, Regis, 86
Kennedy, Robert, 24
King, Martin Luther, Jr., xii, 21
King, R. Edwin, 61, 76
Kisselbasch, Hamid, 61–62
Ku Klux Klan (KKK), xi, xxx, xxxiv

Lampley, James, 87, 88
Land, Joe Louis, 83
Lee, Herbert, xvii, 38, 43
Leflore County, xv, xvi, 10, 12, 14, 29, 101
Lelyveld, Rabbi, 95, 96
Lenard, Judge, 49
Levine, Allan, **106–7**
Little, George, vii
Lowndes County, 69
Loyal Democrats, xxi
Luckett, Vernon O., 93, 99

Madison County, 48, 60, 61, 84
Mandel, Lisa, 104–5
Mandel, Robert, **104–5**

Martinsons, Andre, 65, 58
Marye, Peggy, 14
McComb, MS, 30, 37, 65–58, 92, 109
McDavia, Melvin, 97, 99
McGill, Bertie, **96**
McGill, Larry, 96
McLaurin, Charles, 69, 70
Meridian, MS, xiii, 68, 71–75
Meridian County, xiii
Mississippi Freedom Democratic Party, x, xii, xxi, xxxvi
Mississippi Summer Project, viii, x, xii, xiii, xviii, xix, xxxiv, xxxv, xxxvi, 69, 74, 101, 104
Montgomery County, 20, 22, 27
Montgomery County Jail, 23, 27
Moore, Russell, 4, 5
Moral Man and Immoral Society, xx
Morris, Jesse T., **63–64**
Morton, Eric, **97–100**
Moses, Bob, xi, xiv, 9–11, 100
Moses, Dona, 57
Mt. Zion Methodist Church, 77–80
Mullvain, Marty, 90, 91
Murph, Dr., 102

NAACP, xii, xiv–xvi, xix, xxi, xxiv, xxxvi, 3, 4, 8, 16, 19, 20, 28, 33, 34, 36, 45, 70, 102
Nash, Diane, 4
Natchez Police Department, 55
National Council of Churches, xii, xxxv, xxxvi, 87
National Theater, viii, xi
Neshoba County, xiii, xix, xxxiii, xxxiv, 71, 74–78, 102
Newman, Doris, 111
Niebuhr, Reinhold, xii, xix

O'Neal, Helen, 52
Owen, Dave, 95–96

116 INDEX

Parchman State Penitentiary, 30, 51
Patterson, Susan B., 103, 104
Payne, Bruce, 45
Peacock, Willie, 11, 14, 15, 69–71
Pendleton, Charles L., **89**
Percy, Walker, xxii
Pigee, Vera Mae, xvi, xxiii, **16**
Pike County, xiv, 34–35, 63, 92, 109
Piney Woods, xiii, xix
Ponder, Annell, xvii, **20–26**
Porter, R. S., 73
Press Register, 8
Price, Cecil, xi, xliii
Pruitt, Jimmy, 30

racial violence, viii, ix, xxiv
Rainey, Lawrence, xi, xxix, xliii, 26
Rawlings, Stuart, 90
Reconstruction, x, xxiv, xxxiii
Redding, Saunders, xxiii
Riley, David, xviii, **92–94**

Sachar, Jeffrey, 106
Sayer, Michael, **101–2**
Schwerner, Michael, xi, xii, xiii, xviii, 71–77
Schwerner, Rita L., xiii, **71–76**
segregation, xxiii, xxxiii, xxxvi
Sharkey County, xix, 107, 108
Silver, James, xx
Simpson, Euvester, 20–22, 27, 57
Sitzer, Lewis, **81–82**
Smith, Ben, 50
Smith, Geoffrey R. W., **102**
Smith, R. T., 35
Smith, Steve, 97–100
Southern Christian Leadership Conference (SCLC), xv, 26
South Strikes Back, The, xx

Spairs, Judge, 108
Spears, Lawrence, **95–96**
Starr, Michael F., **77–80**
Steptoe, E. W., xiv, 3–4, 43
Stoner, Peter, **49–51**
Student Nonviolent Coordinating Committee (SNCC), xi, xiii, xiv, xvi, xxi, xxxiv, 9–12, 15, 26, 29, 40, 57, 69, 70, 75, 95, 107
Sunflower County, 11, 20, 106
Supriano, Harold, 33
Surney, Lafayette, **33–34, 110–12**
Sutherland, Charlie, 84, 85

Tallahatchie County, vii, ix, x
Tanner, Beatrice, 12
Till, Emmett, ix, 12
Tougaloo College, 61, 76
Travis, James "Jimmy," xvi, **9–10**, 15
True Light Baptist Church, 103
Turner, Bessie, xvi, xxii, 7

U.S. Department of Justice, 8, 11, 18, 19, 26, 33, 34, 36, 45

Vicksburg, MS, xiii
voter registration, x, xiii, xiv, xvi, xvii, xliv, 3, 9, 20, 23, 26, 29, 30, 49, 50, 52, 57, 77, 81, 84, 95, 97, 98, 101, 104
Voting Rights Act, xxii

Wallace, George, 76
Warren County, xviii, 92, 93
Watts, Joe Lee, 60
Welsh, David P., **61–62**
Werner, Peter C., xviii, **103–4**
West, James, 20–23, 27
Whitaker, A. C., xix
White Citizens' Council, 66
White Knights, xix

Williams, Kidada, xxiv
Winona, MS, xvi, xvii, xxiii, 20, 23, 27, 28
Wright, Marian, 86

Young, Andrew, 26
Young, Eddie, Jr., 82, 83

Zaretsky, Malcolm, 90, 91
Zellner, John Robert, 75, 76

www.ingramcontent.com/pod-product-compliance
Lightning Source LLC
Chambersburg PA
CBHW030556230426
43661CB00054B/2155